shout

the award-winning teen magazine brings
must-have guide to what's going on in you

C000057039

101 Things A Girl Needs To Know!

If you want a crash course in confidence then read on!

101 Things is all about how great it is to be a girl, how to take some positive steps to get the things you really, really want and have some fun along the way! It's packed with beauty and fashion tips, celebrity secrets, advice on coping with all the things that life might throw at you in your teenage years plus how to have a good time!

Fake tan… false friends… bullies… bigmouths… being dumped… saying sorry… smelling sensational… decoding dreams… de-stressing… healthy handbags… high heels… beauty tricks… best mates… first dates… fighting frizz… mocktails… moods…
MAKING THE MOST OF EVERY SINGLE DAY!

If it's in your life — it's in
101 Things A Girl Needs To Know!

contents

beauty

fashion

your world

Printed and published by D.C.Thomson & Co., Ltd., 185 Fleet Street, London EC4A 2HS. © D.C.Thomson, 2008. Whilst every reasonable care will be taken neither D.C.Thomson & Co., Ltd., nor its agents accept liability for loss or damage to colour transparencies or any other material submitted to this publication.

how to…
have
amazing
skin!

Insider info to
make you sparkle!

Scrub...

When your skin's looking a bit under the weather, you can end up feeling a bit like that too! Defeat dull skin and get your hands on a scrub that'll bring some colour back into your cheeks. Dead skin cells can really rain on your complexion parade...

Freshen your face with Neutrogena Pure Glow Warming Scrub.

Mop...

Every morning and night, wipe away the grime that seems to be so annoyingly attracted to your pores and never apply make-up to skin that's anything less than squeaky clean!

Sock it to those spots with Clearasil Deep Pore Treatment Pads.

Polish...

If you've tried eating your five-a-day and taking exercise but your skin is still less glow and more oh no, make like the A-list and cheat! Take your pick from hundreds of fake tan treats then carefully apply after exfoliating and moisturising — you'll be looking tantastic in no time!

Soap & Glory One Night Tanned will give your skin a bronze boost!

clean up *your act*

If your skin's feeling a little worse for wear, have a complexion-friendly spring clean...

Dust...

Even girls with a need for speed will have time for this quick trick that'll get your skin looking sunnier in just seconds! Dust on your fave bronzer! Even if it's only to the apples of your cheeks, it'll give you a bronze boost for the day!

Look hot in a hurry with Barry M Natural Dazzle.

Wash...

Seems pretty obvious but a first-class cleanser is top of the list for a lush complexion! Choose one that'll shift your make-up so you don't have to spend ages rubbing at the sensitive skin around your eyes...

Stop being a *dirrty* girl with Johnson's Eye Make-up Remover.

Sweep...

Finish your spring clean with an oh-so-saintly showdown... Get your paws on a mega-moisturiser that'll give your skin a drink and protect it from the elements at the same time.

Radiant skin comes in a bottle... Face Boutique Fresh Faced Moisturiser.

Turn over for more tips!

All products available at time of press.

7

STAR SKINCARE SORTED…

Kate Nash

Angry spots and acne need gentle treatment, so see your doc and try Avène Cleanance Soapless Gel Cleanser. This mild cleanser with antibacterial active ingredients is perfect!

STAR SKINCARE SORTED…

Posh

Proof that even super stars suffer from bad skin days… Fight back against greasy, oily pimples with oil-free products and gentle treatments. We love Clean & Clear Shine Control Daily Facial Wash.

the HOT skin top 10...

1. The skin around your eyes is extra sensitive and can be the giveaway sign that you're totally tired! Pop cool teabags or cotton wool soaked in milk over your eyes to perk up your peepers!

2. *So you've heard "drink eight glasses of water a day" about a million times but that's because it's more or less true... Other liquids count towards your intake so sip on water, tea and fruit juice to make sure you and your skin stay hydrated!*

3. Even on dull, cloudy days, slap on sun protection — more than half the sun's rays can pass through clouds! Make sure that you apply a sunscreen over your moisturiser every day, even in winter!

4. *Keep your hands away from your face! It might sound obvious but touching your skin can transfer oil and dirt, causing those buggin' blemishes!*

5. Eat your way to a glowing complexion! Oily fish, nuts and seeds are full of essential fatty acids (good for you!)... which help your skin repair itself and stay moisturised. Fruit like blackberries, plums and strawberries are also skin saviours, so fill up!

6. Before you head to bed for your beauty sleep, check your skin's make-up free and moisturised! Make sure to change your pillowcases every few days as they can get grubby whilst you snooze!

7. *Chew your food very slowly to ensure it's properly digested... Undigested food can turn toxic in your system and lead to pimples and cellulite!*

8. You may not always feel like getting active but your skin will thank you for it! A game of footie with the girls (or hot guys?!) or a brisk walk round the shops (with heavy bags!) will get your circulation going and, in turn, help keep your skin and organs supplied with oxygen and nutrients — essential for a fresh, healthy-looking complexion.

9. *Wash your face with warm water, never hot, and rinse with cool water, never cold. For best results, stay away from soap as it can leave residue on your skin, even after rinsing.*

10. Eat a variety of different veggies daily. That way you'll have a good mix of different nutrients to help keep your skin looking flawless. Your plate should be colourful!

Turn over for more tips!

GARNIER
AMBRE SOLAIRE

evian
Natural Mineral Water

9

FAKE *flawless!*

When all else fails, make-up comes to the rescue! Check these tricks for complexion perfection...

1. Keep Clean

Before you start to conceal, make sure your hands are freshly washed to stop bacteria from spreading and clogging up pores. Wash your make-up brushes at least once a month to keep them germ-free, too.

2. Conceal It

Before applying foundation, dot concealer around blemishes, dark circles and spots — the easiest and most effective way is using your fingertips to gently blend. Choose a shade that's slightly lighter than your skin tone... but not too different! Apply around any blemishes then blend in towards the middle for invisible coverage!

3. Foundation Fast

Find the perfect foundation shade by testing on your neck or jawline, not the back of your hand — and always in natural light! Gently blend in your foundation... use fingertips to apply it directly to problem skin areas and, for all-over application, try a foundation brush. Don't forget to check for tell-tale slip-ups around your hairline and chin to make sure your face looks flawless!

4. Powder Power

Set your concealer by patting skin with a face powder. Apply sparingly though — you don't want to look like you're wearing a mask! If your skin feels dry, dust powder around your nose and forehead only.

5. Colour Up

Finish with blush or bronzer to brighten your skintone and add to that airbrushed effect! For a fresh, rosy complexion swirl a pink blush onto the apples of the cheeks (smile to find the right place) and lightly add bronzer to your nose, forehead and temples for a sunkissed look.

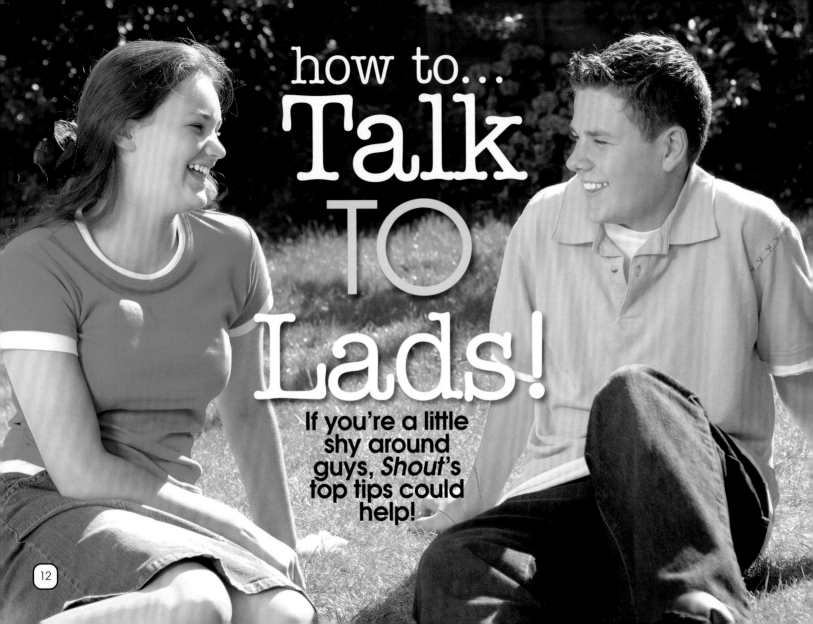

how to...
Talk TO Lads!

If you're a little shy around guys, *Shout*'s top tips could help!

So there's a hot lad in your class who you really like, but you're not sure if he even knows your name? Or maybe there's a funny boy in your year whose jokes you've been laughing at from a distance, and you reckon he'd make a really good mate? Or perhaps there's a really shy guy you've had your eye on for a while and you'd like to get to know him better? Sound familiar?

The fact is that if these guys were actually girls, you'd have no problems initiating a chat with them — but they're not... and you can't. Striking up a conversation with a lad can be a little more challenging, but it's not the most difficult thing in the world — honest! Study **shout**'s top tips and we guarantee that before long, he'll be all ears...

Yeah But No But!

When it comes to attempting to have a chat with a lad, rule number one is to try to avoid asking questions that can be answered with just a simple 'yes' or 'no'. By nature, a lot of guys aren't all that talkative (you might have noticed this before!) and if you throw him a 'So do you like The Kooks?', he'll reply with a 'Yeah, I suppose so' and before the conversation's even started, it'll be over.

Get His Attention!

Now that we've cleared that up, you've got to think of ways to start a conversation. The best way to do this is to use things that you've both got in common. If he's in your class at school, why not ask him what he thought of a recent exam? Or ask him if he finds the teacher's whiny voice quite as annoying as you do!

Talk About *Him*!

Most people like to talk about themselves and their interests, so find out what he's into and get researching it — films, TV shows, bands and sports are all excellent topics. Use the internet to read up on all his favourites and then impress him with your knowledge! Once he sees you "share" his interests, he'll no doubt want to talk to you about them more…

Laughter's the best medicine!

Make Him Laugh!

Everyone loves a good giggle so you shouldn't think twice about showing off your sense of humour! Why not try telling him a funny story you've heard or about something embarrassing (not too cringey, mind!) that's happened to you? You could even try telling him a cheesy joke — if you pull it off he'll have a good chuckle, and if you end up fluffing the punchline, he'll most likely think you're cute for trying!

Don't Ramble!

Now that you've managed to strike up a conversation, it's important not to ruin it by turning into a complete chatterbox! When people are nervous they can sometimes start blabbering on about everything under the sun — so you've got to keep your talking under control! If you start dominating the conversation, rambling on and forgetting to ask questions, he'll think you're not interested in hearing about him and you'll come across as a little self-centred. Plus, you'll end up giving him a massive headache — which rarely leads to a beautiful friendship!

Be Yourself!

Don't forget to be your fabulous self! There's nothing wrong with telling a few little white lies to show that you have more in common than he thinks, but you have to be careful not to go too far. When you're trying to impress someone, it can be really tempting to embellish the truth or exaggerate to make yourself appear more attractive — but the truth is, you're fine the way you are! Believe us, honesty is definitely the best policy because blatant lies always come back to haunt you. Tell him about your friends, family and hobbies — if he's a nice guy, he'll be interested in you for you…

Take Risks!

No matter how pretty, funny or smart you are — no-one gets the response they want every time from someone they're into. There isn't anyone in the world who hasn't experienced rejection before, so don't let this fear hold you back! One thing's for sure — you definitely don't want to be left wondering what might have been if you'd found the courage to talk to him. So get out of your comfort zone, start asking questions and go with the flow — just make sure the lad you're after is worth all the trouble!

Get Flirty!

Don't be afraid to try out your flirting technique! Try grabbing his attention by glancing at him a couple of times each day and give him a big smile when he turns to look at you. When you're talking to him, eye contact is vitally important — so be sure to hold his stare. If you haven't tried flirting before, you'll be surprised at how easy and natural it is to pick up! Have fun — it's totally harmless!

Be confident and don't fear rejection!

SUPER-QUICK
Beauty Tricks!
One-minute makeovers to make you look great!

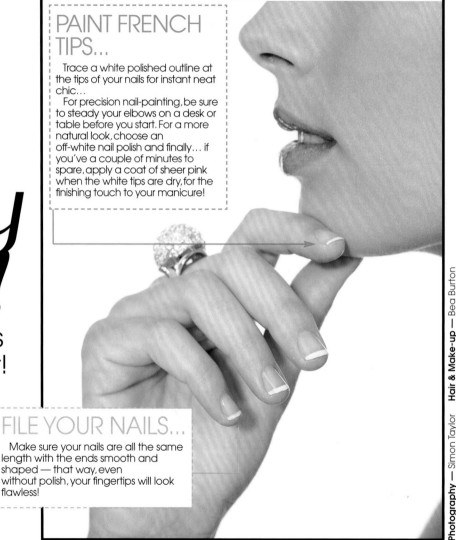

Photography — Simon Taylor   **Hair & Make-up** — Bea Burton

PAINT FRENCH TIPS...

Trace a white polished outline at the tips of your nails for instant neat chic...

For precision nail-painting, be sure to steady your elbows on a desk or table before you start. For a more natural look, choose an off-white nail polish and finally... if you've a couple of minutes to spare, apply a coat of sheer pink when the white tips are dry, for the finishing touch to your manicure!

FILE YOUR NAILS...

Make sure your nails are all the same length with the ends smooth and shaped — that way, even without polish, your fingertips will look flawless!

NAIL KIT...
Elegant Touch Crystal Glass File
Rimmel Nail Tip Whitener

GO FOR GOLD...

Whatever your eye colour, a fingertip-sized smudge of shimmery gold eyeshadow on the inner corners of your eyes will perk up your peepers and make you look stunning in seconds! Ooh!

WORK THAT LIPGLOSS...

Lipgloss is an obvious quick fix but for a plump pout when time is short, add extra shine to the middle of your bottom lip and opt for pink — it's a quick-fix teeth whitener!

GLOSSY GLAM!
Miss Sporty Fabulous Gloss in St Tropez

TRY PEACH BLUSHER...

Swap your rosy pink blush for a peach flush across your cheeks instead and achieve a healthy, sunkissed look! Use a blusher brush and sweep outwards from the apples of your cheeks, fading towards the top of your ears!

GET A GORGEOUS GLOW...
Fake Bake Legal Sunburn in Peach Make-up by Barbara Daly Blusher Brush, Tesco

WEAR DIAMANTÉ EARRINGS...

Yep, we're serious! Diamanté earrings reflect light onto your face, giving your complexion an instant boost and making eyes sparkle! Oversize gem studs during the day and dangling jewels at night are essential!

17

FLIRT WITH PALE EYES...

Go ultra ladylike and make your eyes look bigger with one sneaky eyeshadow secret! On average, the distance between eyelashes and eyebrows on girls is twice that of guys, so by using pale eyeshadow, you'll make the area look bigger. Bigger eyes and extra girlie gorgeousness… what are you waiting for?!

THE PERFECT NUDE...
Natural Collection Single Eyeshadow in Sea Shell, Boots

CURL YOUR LASHES...

Use eyelash curlers to instantly open sleepy eyes! Apply a natural shade of eyeshadow over your whole lid, then curl your lashes. Place the curler at the base of your top lashes and hold for 15 seconds then move the curlers up and squeeze mid-way for extra curl. Finish with dark brown mascara for a smouldering look, any time, anywhere!

BIG-UP YOUR LASHES!
Tweezerman Classic Lash Curler
Max Factor Masterpiece Max Mascara in Black-brown

PINK TO MAKE THE BOYS WINK...

First it was white eyeliner pencil to awaken those tired peepers, but try switching to a pastel pink eyeliner instead for whiter whites that'll get your eyes popping! Apply on the inner corners of your eyes then smudge slightly towards your nose — easy!

EASY TO SMUDGE...
Bourjois Khôl & Contour Eyeliner in Rose Fantaisiste

FLUFF UP YOUR HAIR...

Give your hair quick-as-a-flash, full-on volume by tipping your head upside down, brushing through and misting with hairspray. Once you flip your hair back to normal, it will look *huuuge*! Perfect for lank locks!

HANDBAG HAIR-SAVER!
OSIS Mini Giant Hairspray

ACCESSORIZE YOUR HAIR...

You can make a statement with your hairstyle! Show you're up-to-date with the latest trends by going for floral prints, bows or oversized jewels on hairbands and slides.

FALL IN LOVE WITH LIQUID LINER...

Black, brown, bright blue... liquid liner, even worn with no other make-up, will make your look zing! If you're an expert, try a thin, neat line above lashes, curving out and upwards but if you still need a bit of practise, a thicker line can sometimes be easier to achieve. Finish with plenty of mascara and leave lips bare for maximum effect!

SHOUT ❤S...

GOSH Eye Liner Pen in Black, Superdrug Barry M Liquid Eyeliner in Blue

TAME THOSE BROWS...

Tidy eyebrows instantly frame your face and make your eyes stand out. Don't get tweezer-happy, but do give stray hairs the heave-ho! Try tweezing after a bath or shower so the hairs pull out more easily and don't tweeze above the arch of your brows. Remember to stop regularly and step back from the mirror so you make sure your brows are even and prevent overplucking.

TRY THESE...

Elegant Touch Coloured Tweezers

MAKE A DATE WITH YOUR HIGHLIGHTER...

It looks great on cheeks, shoulders and shins but there's another handy use for highlighter! Carefully dotted on your cupid's bow (just above the middle of your top lip), it'll make your lips look plump 'n' pouty!

SHOW OFF WITH...

MeMeMe Beat The Blues Highlighter

All products available at time of press.

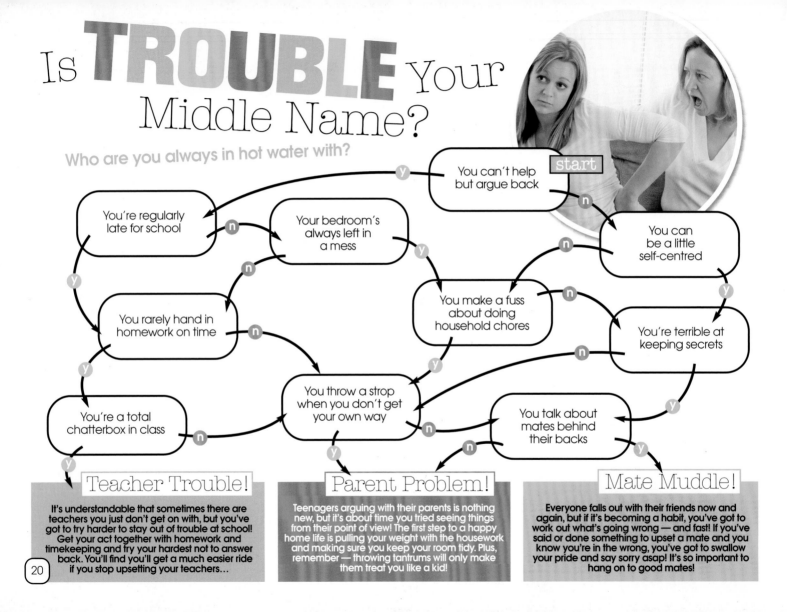

Is **TROUBLE** Your Middle Name?

Who are you always in hot water with?

start

You can't help but argue back

You're regularly late for school

Your bedroom's always left in a mess

You can be a little self-centred

You rarely hand in homework on time

You make a fuss about doing household chores

You're terrible at keeping secrets

You're a total chatterbox in class

You throw a strop when you don't get your own way

You talk about mates behind their backs

Teacher Trouble!

It's understandable that sometimes there are teachers you just don't get on with, but you've got to try harder to stay out of trouble at school! Get your act together with homework and timekeeping and try your hardest not to answer back. You'll find you'll get a much easier ride if you stop upsetting your teachers…

Parent Problem!

Teenagers arguing with their parents is nothing new, but it's about time you tried seeing things from their point of view! The first step to a happy home life is pulling your weight with the housework and making sure you keep your room tidy. Plus, remember — throwing tantrums will only make them treat you like a kid!

Mate Muddle!

Everyone falls out with their friends now and again, but if it's becoming a habit, you've got to work out what's going wrong — and fast! If you've said or done something to upset a mate and you know you're in the wrong, you've got to swallow your pride and say sorry asap! It's so important to hang on to good mates!

20

saying
sorry…
SORTED!

It needn't be the hardest word…

Listen Up

The person you're apologising to might still be feeling angry. They might not even know whether they can ever forgive you (eek!). Let them put their point of view across without butting in. Remember, you're the one in the wrong here!

Mean It!

There's nothing worse than a half-hearted or insincere apology. Don't say sorry for the sake of it — you've got to really mean it. And don't say sorry just to make yourself feel better — this isn't about you, remember?!

JUST DO IT!

Don't put off saying sorry —

if you want to say it,

say it!

Practise!

If you know you've got to say sorry to someone, you can help make things easier by practising in front of a mirror, or even to a friend, sister or your mum! Actually saying the words out loud can make you much less nervous when you finally do the deed!

Take A Deep Breath

Calm your nerves by taking a few deep breaths. Then stand up straight, make lots of eye contact and go for it. You'll be glad you did!

No Ifs, No Buts!

Here's how to phrase your apology — "I'm sorry I hurt your feelings"… NOT "I'm sorry if I hurt your feelings". Accept that you did something wrong, and take the blame!

Don't Make Excuses

Unless you have a proper excuse for doing what you did, then zip it! Nothing's worse than a lousy excuse — it can really devalue an apology.

Put Pen To Paper

Sometimes, if you've had a huge falling out with someone, or you've done something *really* bad, it can seem too daunting to say sorry face-to-face. Maybe you don't know how the other person will react, or even if they'll listen. The way to get round this problem is to write your apology down. That way, the person you're saying sorry to will have time to think about what you've said, and then the ball is in their court — they can choose to accept your apology — or not — and make the next move.

AND THE GOLDEN RULE OF SAYING SORRY…

Whatever it is you've done wrong, make sure you never do it again — that's one less thing to say sorry for in the future!

Dress Like A WAG

If it's good enough for Coleen and VB…

SHADY LADIES...

There's really no better way to get some instant WAG style than by slipping on a pair of sunnies — just look at Victoria! She's made huge sunglasses her trademark, and if you're going to dress like any WAG it might as well be the queen bee, right? The only thing you've got to remember is... the bigger, the better! You'd never catch VB in some teeny tiny specs, even if they *were* super expensive...

Fake? Who, us?

You're probably not surprised that fake tan is the next WAG essential — the pale 'n' pasty look just isn't doing it for them! If you want a tan that would look good next to *Cristiano* then make sure you buff up your skin with loads of body scrub before you start... But be warned — streaks and patchy bits are so D-List!

25

WAGS LOVE BAGS!

A bag is no mere accessory to hot-shot WAGs — having the latest super trendy bag on your arm is almost as cool as having Becks on it! It doesn't matter if your bag's designer — just make sure it's HUGE, slouchy and leather. Coleen's always got about ten different colours of every bag worth having, and check out VB — she's even matched her hot pink Birkin to her dress! Now that's what we call WAG style!

Earn Your Stripes

As for clothes, trackies have always been a fave with WAGs... its velour all the way, and don't be shy when it comes to colour either! Cheryl looks hot in bright green — and some WAGs have even been known to step out in leopard print! Well, you've got to make sure you stand out from the crowd, don't you?

Perma-Glam…

For the rest of the time it's all-out glamour — you want to look like you've spent three hours in front of the mirror, even if you haven't! Heels are essential, but you'll have to say goodbye to pain-free tootsies if you want to look like a WAG because we mean HIGH heels! Skinny jeans are still in, and make sure you've slipped on some bling as well! Just remember, while WAGs like to flash their rocks on their fingers the rest of their jewellery is all pretty dainty and understated (that doesn't mean it's not expensive though!).

It's not only us with copycat style — Cheryl's hair looks strangely like Posh's pob here…

Beauty Checklist:

LIPGLOSS: *Pink please!*
FRENCH MANICURE: *Never be seen without your white tips!*
HAIR STRAIGHTENERS: *Only GHDs will do!*
PERFUME: *It's got to be Coleen or Intimately Beckham, doesn't it?*

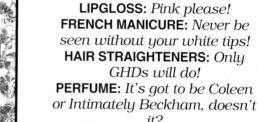

All you need now is a mega-hot footballer! Mmmm… where did **Cristiano** go?

All products available at time of press.

27

how to...
Find The *Perfect Trainers!*
Find your ultimate stylish sneakers!

start → You're a pretty good singer

You're a pretty good singer — no → You're a shopaholic

You're a pretty good singer — yes → Ashlee Simpson is awesome

Ashlee Simpson is awesome — no → You rock the natural look

Ashlee Simpson is awesome — yes → You want to live in L.A. with the stars

You rock the natural look — no → Shopping is your workout

You rock the natural look — yes → You'd be lost without your eyeliner

You're a shopaholic — yes → You've had a manicure

You're a shopaholic — no → Shopping is your workout

You've had a manicure — no → R 'n' B rocks!

You've had a manicure — yes → R 'n' B rocks!

R 'n' B rocks! — no → You'd be lost without your eyeliner

R 'n' B rocks! — yes → Fashion over function!

Shopping is your workout — no → You'd be lost without your eyeliner

Shopping is your workout — yes → Fashion over function!

You want to live in L.A. with the stars — yes → You'd be lost without your eyeliner

You want to live in L.A. with the stars — no → RETRO ROCKS!

You'd be lost without your eyeliner — yes → SPORT STYLE!

You'd be lost without your eyeliner — no → SPORT STYLE!

Fashion over function! — no → SPORT STYLE!

Fashion over function! — yes → FASHION FORWARD!

RETRO ROCKS!

Bags of style without the fuss? Then you ought to check out Converse's range of ultra-cool sneakers! They look really cute and come in a huge range of colours, so you'll have a pair to match every outfit — just what you've always wanted!

SPORT STYLE!

You don't want a pair of trainers — you need them! You spend practically all your time in them, so you need a pair that will give your feet plenty of support. Nike Air are an all-time classic so get your hands (and feet) on a pair now!

FASHION FORWARD!

You think about your style from head to toe before you leave the house so it's a no-brainer that you'd pick the trendy type. Whether you want them in hot pink or sleek 'n' black, adidas has the ultimate range of stylish trainers!

how to...
Keep Your
HANDBAG
HEALTHY

What's lurking in the bottom of yours?

29

FILTHY FACTS:

● In one sample, four out of five handbags tested positive for salmonella!

● A study that tested ten random girls' handbags found that they were ALL covered in germs! One girl's was coated with a gross 6.7 million bacteria! Yuck!

● The people with the dirtiest bags were mothers and people who hung out at clubs all the time. Er… how grubby must celeb mum Nicole Richie's designer handbag be then?

BAG-TERIA:
What Can You Catch?

● INTESTINAL PROBLEMS
● DEHYDRATION
● DIARRHOEA
● EYE INFECTIONS

● COLD VIRUSES
● FOOD POISONING
● SKIN INFECTIONS

DIRTY ON THE OUTSIDE:

● Always use the hooks in loos to hang up your bag — don't just dump it on the floor! Think how gross that is…

● Think of your bag like a pair of super cool sparkly heels. You wouldn't put them on your desk, table or kitchen counter, would you?

● Make sure you wash your bag regularly. Pop cloth bags in the washing machine, and if they're leather or patent you can get them gleaming again with an antibacterial wipe!

DIRTY ON THE INSIDE:

● Did you know your mega glam moby could be filthier than a toilet seat? Loads of bacteria breed on handsets cause they're kept all snug and warm in our bags — so make sure you clean them regularly with an antibacterial wipe!

● In a study, some purses were a whopping 100 times dirtier than the average toilet seat (eek!) — so either pop them in the wash or give them a wipe!

● They don't call it dirty money for nothing, you know! Cash is passed between lots of different people and carries loads of bacteria, so don't put your hands in your mouth after you've touched it!

Is Your
FRIEND A FAKE?

Find out how good your friendship really is!

What's a 'FAKE' FRIEND?

A fake friend is someone who doesn't treat you as well as you should be treated. If she puts you down in front of other people, only gets in touch when there's no-one else around or gossips about you behind your back, she's definitely not good for you!

The golden rule is that your friends should treat you the same way you treat them — they should always be there for you when you need them, give you lots of encouragement and be lots of fun to hang around with.

How do I **spot if my friend's a fake?**

Tick all of the boxes that you agree with:

■ You can't relax when she's around.

■ You prefer to have other mates there when you're with her.

■ You're secretly happy when she cancels your plans.

■ You're moody after you've spoken to her.

■ People find it strange that you're mates.

- -

So, how many boxes did you tick?

3 or more
It's definitely time to ditch her!

1 or 2
It's time to take a good look at your friendship.

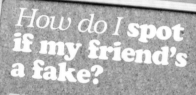

Turn over for more!

FAKE FRIENDS...

- Spill your secrets!
- Steal your boyf!
- Stand you up!
- Embarrass you in front of others!
- Love talking about themselves!
- Don't care about your problems!

FAB FRIENDS...

- Listen when you talk!
- Share secrets... but only with each other!
- Support you when you've got a problem!
- Tell you you look fab!
- Always turn up when they say they will!
- Ask your crush out for you when you're too shy!

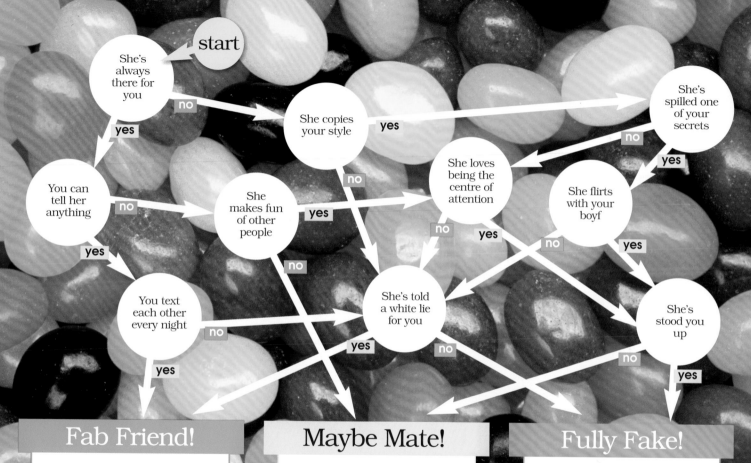

start

She's always there for you
- yes → You can tell her anything
- no → She copies your style

You can tell her anything
- no → She makes fun of other people
- yes → You text each other every night

She copies your style
- yes → She's spilled one of your secrets
- no → She's told a white lie for you

She makes fun of other people
- yes → She loves being the centre of attention
- no → She's told a white lie for you

You text each other every night
- no → She's told a white lie for you
- yes → **Fab Friend!**

She loves being the centre of attention
- no → She's told a white lie for you
- yes → She's stood you up

She's spilled one of your secrets
- no → She loves being the centre of attention
- yes → She flirts with your boyf

She flirts with your boyf
- no → She's told a white lie for you
- yes → She's stood you up

She's told a white lie for you
- yes → **Maybe Mate!**
- no → **Maybe Mate!**

She's stood you up
- no → **Maybe Mate!**
- yes → **Fully Fake!**

Fab Friend!

There's nothing fake about this mate! She's totally trustworthy and you can always depend on her. In fact, the two of you are so close that you could be sisters!

Maybe Mate!

She's lots of fun to be around but you know you can't always rely on her — she's more of a casual friend than best mate material!

Fully Fake!

Oh dear! This girl's no mate at all! She'll do anything to be popular… even if it means hurting you in the process. Steer clear!

35

how to... smell scent-sational!

shout *knows how to make you a perfume pro!*

Tick the boxes to discover which type of perfume suits you perfectly...

- ■ Girlie dresses and skirts are my wardrobe favourites.
- ■ I've been known to borrow my friends' clothes.
- ■ I don't understand boys — they just annoy me.
- ■ I've got loads of mates and keep in touch with old friends too.
- ■ I splash my cash on impulse buys — saving up is too hard!
- ■ I'm super-organised — nothing gets past me!
- ■ I've got one close mate who knows all my secrets.
- ■ I love fun films like *Step Up 2* rather than scary movies.
- ■ I'd always wear heels if my feet could handle it!
- ■ I'd love to be in a girl band like **Girls Aloud** — how much fun!
- ■ I'd rather go to the cinema than to a nightclub.
- ■ Okay, I like to practise flirting... so?!
- ■ An outfit isn't complete until I've got my bling on!
- ■ Exams? There's no point stressing out and studying all night beforehand.
- ■ I love trying new clothes combinations to get a really individual look.
- ■ Skiving P.E. is a waste of time, I like sport!
- ■ People say I'm a chatterbox... I just have lots to say!
- ■ I'm happy shopping on my own... it's easy to spot great buys that way!
- ■ If someone tried to bully my mate, they'd have to go past me first!
- ■ I never say no to a party invite!

Which colour did you pick the most? Turn over to find out what it reveals about you...

Mostly pink...

You're girlie and gorgeous with an impulsive streak... you love getting dressed up and can find any excuse to go glam! A scent to match your pretty personality would just have to be pink!

You'd ❤...

Hugo Boss Essence De Femme

Lacoste Touch of Pink

Paris Hilton Heiress

Mostly purple...

You're independent, cool and always calm under pressure, in fact you're the first port of call for any friend in need of sound advice — you always know the answer! Stand out in a dramatic perfume that'll turn heads!

You'd ❤...

Chanel Coco Mademoiselle

Kate by Kate Moss

Vivienne Westwood Let It Rock

Mostly blue...

Sometimes shy and never one to steal the limelight, you're a behind-the-scenes kinda girl and a super-loyal mate who won't let your friends down... ever!

Go for a scent that's warm and friendly, just like you!

You'd ♥...

DKNY Be Delicious

Anna Sui Flight Of Fancy

Kylie Minogue Showtime

Mostly green...

You're the social butterfly and Little Miss Popular amongst your friends — you can round up your mates in record time when you've got a party planned!

Smell sensational in something fresh and fabulous...

You'd ♥...

Diesel Fuel For Life

Island Michael Kors

Roxy Love

All products available at time of press.

how to...
Stand Up For Yourself!

Go on... you can do it!

No-one really likes confrontation but there are times in life that we all have to stand up for ourselves. Whether it's over a silly argument or something important, you have to speak up and be strong if you believe that you're right. Yep, a lot of the time it's easier just to give in and let other people get their own way, but this often means that you end up missing out on something or, worse, even becoming a victim! The first couple of times you do it, defending yourself can be pretty nerve-wracking, but it's worth it in the end! You don't have to be rude or aggressive — standing up for yourself is actually pretty easy! Here's how...

Your Mates

No matter how well you and your mates get on, you're always going to disagree every now and again. Most of the time this will be over trivial stuff — your best friend has bought the same top as you, she says she's a bigger Zac Efron fan than you, she forgets your birthday — pretty normal stuff! However, what do you do when you have a major fall out…?

If you're in the wrong, don't be too proud to say sorry!

What To Do

Well, if you know you're the one in the wrong, then swallow your pride and apologise! After all, do you really want to lose her friendship?

However, if you know that you're right then hopefully she'll apologise pretty quickly. If she doesn't, then it's time to stand your ground. It might be that she just avoids you, and goes off with other friends. Yep, it's a shame but give it time and it could blow over.

Unfortunately, things can sometimes turn pretty nasty when mates fall out. From talking about you behind your back to turning other friends against you or even to actual bullying, ex-mates can do a lot of damage! If this happens to you, you need to get it sorted — quickly! Here's how:

● Try to ignore her. Is she worth the hassle…?
● If she won't let up, take her aside and tell her that you know you're no longer friends but want her to stop spreading stories about you. Stay calm — don't let her wind you up!

● Talk to your other mates and explain the whole story to them. You can't force them to believe you over her but, if you handle it calmly enough, they're more likely to take your side.

● If things get worse, confide in an adult — your parents or a teacher. Keep them informed as to what's going on so they can monitor the situation in case it gets out of control.

Your Parents

It's a fact of life that all teenagers argue with their parents now and again… or even every day! You probably feel that they're still treating you like a kid when you know you're nearly an adult. The thing is, though, that in their eyes you *are* still their little girl! It's hard for parents to accept the fact that their children are growing up, which means that the more you try to become independent of them, the harder they try to hold on to you.

What To Do

Firstly, and most importantly, don't throw a strop every time you think they're being too strict. If you act like a child, they'll treat you like a child!

Stamping your feet or slamming doors won't get you very far, no matter how much you want to let off steam!

Instead of the tantrum, take a deep breath and talk to them (don't shout!) about the situation calmly. Explain things from your side. Communicating with your parents calmly and rationally will show them that you can deal with things as an adult, so they're more likely to react positively… which means you've got a better chance of getting what you want!

Stay calm… and stay in control!

Your Teachers

Even if you totally love school, there's bound to be teachers that you don't really get on with. Whether that's cos you don't like the subject or just don't like her, there could be times when you clash or you feel that she's picking on you.

What To Do

- Don't argue back! Your teacher might see this as you being cheeky so you'll end up in even more trouble!
- Stay back at the end of the class and ask to have a word with your teacher. Explain (calmly!) that you think she treated you unfairly and that you'd like to give her your side of the story. Stay respectful and she's likely to give you a chance to explain, so you can sort things out.
- If you keep on having problems with her, then ask your head of year or guidance teacher to help. Don't just assume they'll take your teacher's side — they're there for you, too!

Don't be scared to ask for help!

Control Is Crucial!

No matter what situation you're in, there's one major thing to remember — don't shout or lose your temper! The minute you get angry or raise your voice, people around you will just think you're out of control and will either stop listening or shout back, which means you won't get anywhere. Keeping calm is the key — stay cool and you're more likely to get your message across… and get your own way!

Bullies

Being bullied is one of the scariest things ever! Even verbal abuse like name calling or whispering behind your back can be really stressful, but if you're being bullied physically, it's terrifying!

What To Do

● Try to make sure you're never in a situation where the bully can get you alone. Get your mates to stay with you all the time at school, even when you go to the loo! Most bullies won't take on a whole group of girls.

● Stay out of her way as much as you can. If she can't see you, she can't bully you!

● Confide in a trusted teacher and get their support. Once the school knows what's going on, they can monitor the situation and take action if the bullying continues.

● Tell your parents. Let them know what's going on so they can talk to your headmaster if your school doesn't do enough to stop the bullying.

how to...
stay safe
ONLINE!

shout reveals the scary
side of surfing the net…

Has the internet replaced diaries and phone conversations in your life? Discussing mates, dates and all things girlie online may not be as safe as you think…

blogs

Blog is short for weblog and is an online diary that can be viewed by almost anyone on the web. Bloggers often add photos, music files and weblinks, too.

BE SAFE...

● Don't give out personal information such as name, address, age, school and clubs.

● Try using a nickname, instead of your real name, to identity your blog.

● Think before putting photos online. Is this something you want the whole world to see?

● Ask permission from friends and family before putting pics of them online.

● Make sure your profile's protected before you start your blog and only accept friends who you actually know!

fact! There are more than 112 million blogs worldwide!

bullying

Online bullying or cyber bullying is an ever-increasing problem. Bullying often transfers from the school playground straight to chatrooms.

BE SAFE...

● It's important to report any abuse to the Internet Service Provider or those managing the chatroom. They can ban the abuser's account or provide you with help.

● If you're at school, let a teacher know what's happening. Don't suffer in silence. Teachers are trained in how to deal with situations like this and know what to do.

● Make sure you keep a history of any bullying, including what was said, names and times and any contact details.

fact! 33% of teenagers in America admitted to being a victim of cyber bullying, while 17% admitted to bullying another individual online.

chatrooms

These days lots of people spend ages chatting in online chatrooms as opposed to face-to-face! Online chatrooms are for small groups of people and feature a web page which you can type text into.

BE SAFE...

● Don't visit private chatrooms for one-to-one chats. It's not only more fun but it's also safer to stay in public chatrooms.

● Avoid random, unregulated chatrooms and only visit those that are moderated.

● Always remember that you can never be sure who it is you're talking to. Adults often pose as kids in chatrooms and will offer to exchange personal info, such as addresses and phone numbers. This action could put you and your family at risk.

fact!

In America 60% of teens said they'd received an e-mail or an instant message from a stranger. 63% of them said they'd replied.

meeting up

You're too old for that 'Never talk to strangers' line, right? Wrong! Most people, who have made friends on the internet will want to meet them at some point in real life. However, not all meetings go to plan…

fact!
36% of teens have friends online whom they have never met in person.

BE SAFE…

● You should NEVER go alone to meet someone who you have met over the internet.

● **You may be convinced the person you're going to meet is trustworthy but anyone you meet online is a stranger. If you must meet the person then go with a parent or take at least one friend with you. Also, let someone else know where you are going and take your mobile phone with you.**

● If you are too scared to tell your parents about meeting your online friend, then this is usually a sign that deep down, you know it's dangerous.

● **Create buddy lists (online address books). You can 'ban', 'ignore' or 'remove' people who annoy you and it's a good way of managing your online friendships.**

Eat Well, Feel Fab!

It's easy to stay healthy — we show you how!

Healthy Eating's Important Cos It...

- *Keeps you looking great!*
- *Makes it easier to fight off nasty illnesses!*
- *Gives you lots of energy!*
- *Helps you concentrate!*
- *Reduces the problem of obesity!*

Think that the best way to lose weight is to skip meals? Wrong! The less you eat the slower your metabolism becomes, which means it'll take you longer to lose weight!

Healthy Eating Means...

- Eating regularly! You should have three meals a day — breakfast, lunch and dinner — as well as healthy snacks in between meals.

- **Ditching the junk food! Fast food, crisps and chocolate are full of saturated fats that not only make you put on weight, but are also really bad for your body. In fact, too much saturated fat can lead to serious heart problems when you're older — yikes!**

- Not skipping meals! If you go without food for too long, your blood sugar levels drop so you'll feel weak, dizzy and unable to concentrate, which isn't much fun!

- **Drinking lots of water! Our bodies are made up of around 75% water, so it's important to stay hydrated, otherwise you could become tired and lethargic. Try adding diluting juice if you don't like plain water or even have a glass of fruit juice.**

Turn over for more!

Snack Attack!

If you get an attack of the munchies, don't reach for the biscuit tin! Try some of these filling, delish and healthy alternatives:

- *A handful of dried nuts or fruit.*
- *A piece of fresh fruit. Why not experiment with fruit you've never tried before, or blend your faves together to come up with an exciting, tasty smoothie?*
- *A cereal bar.*
- *Rice pudding — you could even add some fruit for extra flavour!*

You don't have to give up your fave takeaway altogether! Having a burger or pizza once a week is fine — after all, everyone needs a treat!

It's Easy!

Healthy eating doesn't have to be boring! There are loads of tasty foods to tempt your tastebuds, and you'll have lots of fun trying out new flavours along the way. Here are some ideas to get you started...

Swap...	For...
Fizzy drinks	*Fruit juice/water*
Double cheeseburger	*Veggie burger*
Deep crust pizza	*Thin crust pizza*
White bread	*Wholemeal bread*
Crisps	*Rice snacks*
Ice cream	*Frozen yoghurt*
Sugary cereal	*Bran/muesli*
Creamy pasta sauce	*Tomato pasta sauce*

how to...
have the
perfect
wardrobe!

These brill basics will make you a style sensation in no time!

To get the best out of your wardrobe you should clean out your clutter before you start. Arrange your clothes into three piles — one for the clothes you're keeping, one for fashion disasters that have probably been lurking in the back (these can be donated to a charity shop), and another pile for good clothes that just don't fit any more. You can give these to a friend or try selling them on eBay for a small profit.

Now you're ready to start building the perfect wardrobe...

plain jane

A plain T-shirt is a wardrobe staple. Luckily, they're as cheap as chips so you can treat yourself to new ones every season! Buy them in a variety of colours and try dressing them up with necklaces or a scarf.

Baker by Ted Baker at Debenhams

Primark

Primark

www.boohoo.com

River Island

Matalan

www.boohoo.com

www.boohoo.com

white shirt chic

A crisp, white shirt is exactly what your wardrobe needs! But it doesn't have to look boring. Bows, ruffles and pinstripes give a cute 'n' quirky edge to your look. Just make sure you wear a white or nude bra underneath!

superskinny

Skinny jeans are here to stay! They're perfect for wearing day or night and can be worn with whatever shoes you like. There's nothing the skinny jean can't do!

Crafted at Republic

Quiz

Primark

Crafted at
Republic

Tammy at
BHS

Generation 915
at New Look

supersize

Dress-down casual just wouldn't be the same without a pair of baggy jeans! For all-out comfort, get yourself a pair of boyfriend jeans or, for a more sophisticated style, a bootcut shape will show off your figure.

55

denim diva

New Look

The denim skirt is an all-year style item! Wear with patterned tights and boots in winter and bare all in summer. Everything will match your denim mini!

Jane Norman

George
at Asda

Red Herring at
Debenhams

Peacocks

Primark

cosy cardigans

A cardigan is essential for any style siren! Wear over a dress for the understated look or combine with your fave jeans and T-shirt for laid-back, indie chic. Whatever your look — a cardi will keep you cosy and stylish!

dress to impress

A dressy top will go far! Don't be shy with the glitter and sequins, and why not try different styles like strapless, v-neck and wrapover? Skinny jeans and heels will go perfectly!

H&M

Bay Trading

we ♥ LBDs!

The little black dress has been in fashion since the beginning of time, so don't ignore the classiest fashion trend around — get one in your wardrobe! A sash or belt will brighten up your look and feel free to add as much or as little bling as you like!

Sophie at mkone

Miss C at Tesco

New Look

boot-ique!

They get worn for half the year, so make sure you invest in a good pair of winter boots. Pick black or brown so you can mix 'n' match your style. Tuck 'em into jeans or wear patterned tights for the ultimate fashion gal look.

Shoe Express

New Look

Primark

Faith

New Look

pump it up!

No wardrobe would ever be complete without a pair of pumps! They should match most items in your already perfect wardrobe. Bows, patent and metallic will keep your feet flat and funky!

61

Office

Primark

atmosphere®

heel we go!

Towering platforms might look totally glam on the Olsen twins — but could you seriously walk in them? If the answer's no then why not try a pair of wedges? The thicker the heel, the more support your foot has. If you're still not confident then an ankle strap ought to keep you in place.

Odeon

Internacionale

grab your coat!

Buy a jacket in a plain colour and you can wear pretty much anything you like with it. Dress it up with colourful scarves and a gorgeous bag. Plus, details like big buttons and a belt give it a funked-up edge.

Tammy
at BHS

going under...

Good style isn't just about what's on the outside — you'll also need to invest in some quality undies. You'll always need a white and black bra so make sure they fit really well. And nude bras might look horrible but they're a godsend — you can't see them under white clothes!

For a NVPL (non-visible pant line) try seamless pants. They're totally comfy and you get them in a huge range of colours.

www.figleaves.com

mkone

No Romeo at
www.figleaves.com

Miss C at
Tesco

Matalan

QS

Internacionale

Tammy at
BHS

Primark

Primark

in the bag

For A-list, day-time chic opt for a large bag. Shimmering colours will keep your outfit looking fresh, and why not try some patent for a glossy, celeb finish?

At night, don't be afraid to stand out from the crowd with an over-the-top glam clutch bag! You can add the strap for hands-free fashion!

accessorise me!

There's absolutely no limit to how you accessorise! Long pendants add girlie charm, and bold gems will get you noticed! Our fave is a big cocktail ring — they make a style statement all on their own!

All products available at time of press.

New Look

www.boohoo.com

www.boohoo.com

Tom Wolfe at Envy

Internacionale

Dorothy Perkins

Dorothy Perkins

Accessorize

Diva at Miss Selfridge

Tammy at BHS

how to...
Smile *Like a* Celeb
These stars won't let anything get them down...

● Juicy pink gloss will perfect that pout!

Paris Hilton

It's not always easy being Paris Hilton... *People think she just parties all the time and don't take her career seriously at all! But even when she falls out with her celeb mates or her latest movie bombs, you'll never see her with anything but a mega-watt smile on her face! So if you haven't done too well in an exam or aren't getting on with a mate, be like* Paris *and don't let it get you down! It's not the end of the world, we promise!*

Cheryl Cole

You'd never guess that **Cheryl Cole** had boy trouble by the size of that grin! Yes, her hubby treated her badly but she wasn't going to let anyone catch her looking down — no way! Instead, **Cheryl** hung out with her **Girls Aloud** mates and made sure she looked AMAZING every single time she left the house! Well, it definitely beats listening to miserable emo songs and crying into a pillow, doesn't it?

● Hang out with your mates for guaranteed laughs!

Leona Lewis

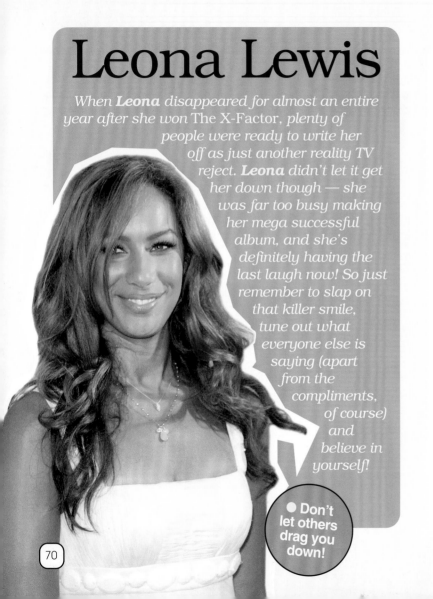

When **Leona** disappeared for almost an entire year after she won The X-Factor, plenty of people were ready to write her off as just another reality TV reject. **Leona** didn't let it get her down though — she was far too busy making her mega successful album, and she's definitely having the last laugh now! So just remember to slap on that killer smile, tune out what everyone else is saying (apart from the compliments, of course) and believe in yourself!

● Don't let others drag you down!

Miley Cyrus

We all make mistakes from time to time, but when **Miley Cyrus** bared a little too much skin in a posh magazine the fall out was so massive we wondered if her career would recover... As it turns out, it was nothing more than a little blip! **Miley** apologised and smiled her way through the scandal, and if she can pull it off, so can you! If you find yourself in a similar situation (okay, not that similar...), just make sure you own up and do whatever you can to make up for it — we're sure you'll be fine!

● Even if you're not feeling too hot, a simple smile could cheer you up — try it!

it's a date!

So that cute guy has *finally* asked you out — here's how to make that first date go brilliantly!

where to go!

It's best to have a plan before you meet up! It depends what you both like doing, what time of day you're going out at and even what the weather's like, but here are some suggestions to get you started:

● **A trip to the cinema:**
Always a winner if you're worried you won't have much to talk about, because you can watch the film and then speak about it afterwards!

● **Dinner:**
Ooh, get you! No, we don't mean a three-course banquet somewhere swanky... how about Pizza Hut instead?!

● **Ice skating or bowling:**
Both are fun and help to break the ice, because you can have a laugh at how bad you are at it!

what to wear!

First date fashion is a minefield! This is not the time to try out a brand new look, girls! The rules are: it's got to fit well, be comfortable and look good. There's nothing worse than tugging at your skirt or fiddling with your bra straps all evening — *so* not a good look! Remember to dress appropriately for the kind of date you're going on — if it's a night at the bowling alley, do you really want to be leaning over in a super-short mini?!

Make-up's important, too. If you don't wear a lot usually, don't start now! You want to look like yourself, and your date wants you to look like you, too! A little bit of mascara, some concealer and a hint of rosy blush will make you look pretty as a picture! And don't forget a swipe of lipbalm for kissable (fingers crossed!) lips! Skip the gooey lipgloss — boys are scared of it!

what to say!

It sounds sad, but it helps to have a few possible conversation topics in your head, just in case it dries up completely! Your date might be super-shy, so be prepared to help things along a little.

● Do your homework and find out what he's interested in, then swot up before the date. We're not asking you to memorise the offside rule, but show a little interest, get a lot back!

● Other possible ice breakers are school, films, music, holidays and hobbies. If in doubt, just ask him loads of questions (but don't make it seem like an interview!) — everyone likes people taking an interest in them.

what happens next...

Well, hopefully your guy will be begging you for a second, third and fourth date! If you follow our tips and play it cool, you've done everything you can to make your first date go fantastically. But remember, some things just aren't meant to be, so if it doesn't go well or you don't hit it off, don't beat yourself up about it. Just get ready for your next first date with someone new!

If things did go well, remember to swap numbers. Don't waste time waiting for a call or text, though — boys are notoriously slow when it comes to following up a date, but if he likes you, he will call eventually!

There's nothing left to say, **shout** girls, except... GOOD LUCK!

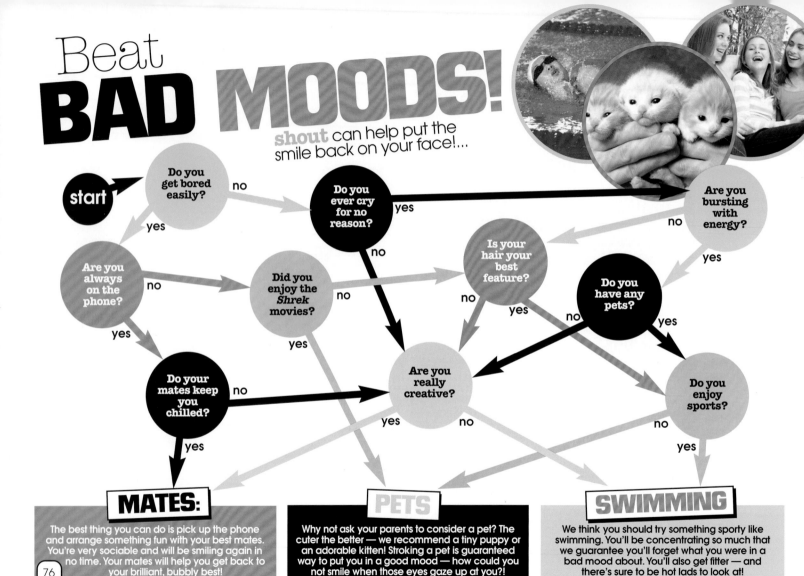

Beat BAD MOODS!

shout can help put the smile back on your face!...

start → Do you get bored easily?

Do you get bored easily? — no → Do you ever cry for no reason?
Do you get bored easily? — yes → Are you always on the phone?

Do you ever cry for no reason? — yes → Are you bursting with energy?
Do you ever cry for no reason? — no → Are you really creative?

Are you always on the phone? — no → Did you enjoy the *Shrek* movies?
Are you always on the phone? — yes → Do your mates keep you chilled?

Did you enjoy the *Shrek* movies? — no → Is your hair your best feature?
Did you enjoy the *Shrek* movies? — yes

Are you bursting with energy? — no
Are you bursting with energy? — yes

Is your hair your best feature? — no
Is your hair your best feature? — yes

Do you have any pets? — no → Are you really creative?
Do you have any pets? — yes → Do you enjoy sports?

Do your mates keep you chilled? — no → Are you really creative?
Do your mates keep you chilled? — yes → **MATES**

Are you really creative? — yes
Are you really creative? — no

Do you enjoy sports? — no
Do you enjoy sports? — yes → **SWIMMING**

MATES:

The best thing you can do is pick up the phone and arrange something fun with your best mates. You're very sociable and will be smiling again in no time. Your mates will help you get back to your brilliant, bubbly best!

PETS

Why not ask your parents to consider a pet? The cuter the better — we recommend a tiny puppy or an adorable kitten! Stroking a pet is guaranteed way to put you in a good mood — how could you not smile when those eyes gaze up at you?!

SWIMMING

We think you should try something sporty like swimming. You'll be concentrating so much that we guarantee you'll forget what you were in a bad mood about. You'll also get fitter — and there's sure to be hot lads to look at!

how to... *get the* perfect blowdry!

A step-by-step perfection plan for gorgeous hair!

Step 1

After washing your hair, finish with a quick rinse with cool water to help smooth your locks before you've even stepped out of the shower!

Step 2

Start drying your hair by gently patting with a towel — don't blowdry hair that's too wet.
Try wrapping your locks in a towel whilst you apply make-up/make breakfast — not only will you be saving time, you'll also find your hair is much easier to blowdry when it's not as wet.

Turn over for more steps!

Step 3

Before you blowdry, apply a product to suit your hair needs…

● **DRY/DAMAGED:** Go for a leave-in conditioner, spray throughout the lengths and ends but steer clear of roots to avoid weighing hair down.

● **CURLY:** Use a straightening balm or serum to help control — rub between your palms and apply evenly.

● **FRIZZY:** Try a serum on damp hair for a more controlled cut…

● **LONG:** Keep volume with a lifting mousse and look after lengths with a heat protection spray.

● **FLAT/OILY:** A volumising mousse or spray ruffled into roots and lengths will work wonders!

A blob of blowdry cream will usually help control most styles — simply rub between palms and run through your hair.

Step 4

Use a wide-toothed comb to spread product evenly through the lengths of your hair and get rid of tangles. Start combing from the bottom of your hair to minimise damage and never use a brush or fine combs as they can split and break hair more easily when it's wet.

Step 5

Invest in a great brush to use whilst blowdrying. Spending that little bit more really can make the difference between a brilliant blowdry and a boring one! A round brush is your best bet to create shine, volume and movement — perfect!

Best buy: ghd Size 3 Anti Static Brush

Step 6

Ideally, your hair should be 70% dry before blowdrying. Not only does this mean your hair will dry faster but it will also suffer less from the heat of the dryer. Use a nozzle to direct air down the length of your hair to encourage the hair to lie more smoothly, and use hair clips to section off your hair so you can reach the strands underneath and ensure your hair is 100% dry!

Step 7

If you have the time (and patience), dry your hair using the slightly cooler setting on your hairdryer and finish with a blast from the cold shot to set your style.

Step 8

Make sure hair is dry, then apply a shine spray or serum (best for thicker styles) and finish with a mist of hairspray to hold.
Ta-da! Salon-perfect hair or what?!

Salon Style
Checklist:

- Hairdryer with nozzle
- Sectioning clips
- Blowdry cream
- Thickening spray
- Wide-toothed comb
- Big round brush
- Shine spray or serum
- Hairspray

All products available at time of press.

Mocktail Time!

They're the latest celeb craze! Let your imagination run wild!

If you want to quench your thirst then mocktails are just the thing for you! They're the 'it' drink — refreshing, fruity and alcohol-free! Here's how to make them...

You'll need:

You can use any type of fruit and juice to make a mocktail... but if you want to start with the most popular ones, you should make sure you've got:

- Cocktail shaker (available in supermarkets)
- Fruit
- Cola
- Grenadine syrup (sweet stuff sold in supermarkets)
- Ginger ale
- Garnishes (umbrellas, straws etc)
- Ice
- Your imagination

Let's get started...

Pineapple Passion **is the current celeb fave so why not try this one first? You'll need four ounces (eight tbsp) of pineapple juice, two ounces of passion fruit juice, one tsp of lemon and one tsp of grenadine. You should mix all the ingredients in a cocktail stirrer/shaker and pour into a glass before adding ice (preferably crushed). All you need to do then is decorate the glass, stir well and enjoy!...**

Turn over to find more mocktail recipes to try!

Here are some other famous mocktails for you to try out:

Dolce & Gabbana: diet cola and grenadine — i.e. – DC & G!

Berry Patch: blueberries, strawberries, raspberries, vanilla ice cream and milk.

Mock Champagne: apple juice, ginger ale and lemon juice.

Pomme Noir: apple juice and cola.

Roy Rogers: cola and grenadine, garnished with a maraschino cherry.

Boston Cooler: ginger ale and vanilla ice cream — this one was invented in Detroit in the 1880s!

Shirley Temple: ginger ale, grenadine and orange juice.

Vienna Soother: coffee, cream, chocolate syrup and cinnamon — maybe your parents would like this one. Think of the brownie points!

Patrick Sweeney: Red Bull, cranberry juice, cola and orange Gatorade or Powerade.

Good luck and remember to let us know if you come up with any amazing recipes!

Find A *Stylish* School Bag!

Stash your stuff... in style!

start

You recycle
- no →
- yes ↓

You won't give up style for school
- yes →
- no ↓

You'd never use a plastic bag
- no →
- yes ↓

You're low maintenance
- no ↓
- yes ↓

Fashion makes your world go round!
- no →
- yes ↓

You play sports every day
- no ↓
- yes ↓

You ♥ make-up
- yes ↓
- no →

You're an eco chick!
- no →
- yes ↓

You're creative
- yes ↓
- no ↓

P.E.'s your fave subject
- no ↓
- yes ↓

Shopper
You're an environmentally-friendly kinda girl, so an eco-tastic tote will double as a school bag and a shopping bag — you're saving the world *and* looking stylish!

Oversized Handbag
You'd much rather use your everyday handbag to carry around your school stuff — you refuse to compromise on style just cos you're at school! And why should you...?!

Sports Bag
You're fit 'n' fab and you need a bag that'll hold your books and your P.E. kit — so choose a sports bag! With loads of pockets for all your essentials, it's the perfect solution!

83

How to get what you want out of life!

Make The Most Of Every Day!

Stop The Snooze!

It's so tempting to hit the snooze button when your alarm goes off every morning, but did you know that snoozing actually makes you more tired? Yep, dozing off and on makes it harder for your body to kick into action, so jump out of bed as soon as your alarm goes off and get ready to start the day.

Be Positive!

No matter how hard things might be, don't let them get you down. It's much harder to deal with problems when you feel sad or stressed, and you can actually end up making them seem worse than they are! Instead of worrying about the situation, try instead to focus on a way to solve it. Picture how relieved and happy you'll be when it's all over and use that positive feeling to help you to cope with what's going on.

Get Your Beauty Sleep!

Celebs swear by it — one of the main ways to look fabulous is to make sure you get enough sleep every night! If you're tired it shows — pale skin, dark circles under your eyes, lifeless hair… yuck! Make sure you get your eight hours every night — your body will thank you for it!

Don't forget, too, that lack of sleep will make you feel grouchy and unable to concentrate… how are you meant to have fun if you're too tired to do any-

Eat Healthily!

It's simple — eat well, look great! Your body needs a healthy, balanced diet in order to stay at its peak, so reducing the amount of junk food and replacing it with things like fruit and veg will give you shiny hair and healthy skin. Aim for at least five portions of fruit and veg a day. If you're not a huge fan of fruit, why not whip up a yummy smoothie to help you along the way?

You'll also find that eating more healthily will mean you've got bags more energy to go out there and have bags more fun!

Smile!

No matter how sad you feel, forcing yourself to smile will instantly make you feel better! If you allow yourself to mope you'll only end up feeling worse. So, whatever's getting you down, try a bit of positive thinking and get those smile muscles working!

Be Brave!

We all like our daily routines — get up, go to school, come home and watch TV, MSN our mates then head to bed... It's easy to fall into a comfort zone but this means we're likely to get pretty bored pretty quickly. Setting yourself new challenges will make life much more interesting! Whether it's a new kind of food, trying to make a new mate, asking your crush out, doing a sponsored run, organising a school trip... think of things you've always fancied trying and start working on them! You'll open your life up to lots of new experiences and probably make some new friends along the way!

Always Do Your Best!

From boring stuff like tidying your room or doing homework for a subject that you totally hate, to making time for your mate when she's got a problem, taking part in important sporty competitions or even just making that special effort for a party, always give it 100%. Knowing you've done the best that you can possibly do will give you a fab sense of satisfaction and inner pride… which will make you shine on the outside, too!

Avoid Arguments

Well, as much as you can anyway! We all know there are times when you're gonna disagree with your mum, your sister, your mate… but make sure that if you do fight, it's for a good reason. Petty arguments are such a waste of energy! Sometimes it's better just to bite your tongue and let it blow over — go on, you can do it!

Love Yourself!

Don't spend time putting yourself down and obsessing about your looks, your weight, the fact you can't chat to lads… As much as we'd all love to look like Rihanna, the fact is that most of us are just pretty normal. Besides, don't forget that all those glam celebs have a team of make-up artists, hairdressers and stylists who follow them around! Learn to love yourself — accept yourself for who you are and focus on your good points instead.

87

hot nails!

Hands up who wants fabulous fingertips?!

Style Secret… Try sprinkling on a pinch of glitter or invest in a body art kit with stick-on jewels that'll look hot on glamorous dark nails.

Top Tip… Give your nails a break. After wearing coloured polish, go for a few days without any polish to refresh!

step 1: file

Start your manicure by removing any old polish, then cut your nails to a neat end-of-your-finger length and file them into a square shape. File your nails in one direction to avoid splitting them. Follow by buffing nails to smooth them off — flaking is a major culprit behind chipped polish! Before applying anything to your nails, make sure you wash your hands to get rid of dirt or oil on nails.

step 2: base

Always apply a base coat to protect your nails… especially before applying coloured polish! It'll stop nails from staining — yuck!

Top Tip… Don't file your nails after a bath or shower as they'll be weaker and more likely to break.

Style Secret… Sunny colours look best on short nails — perfect if you're growing bitten tips!

step 3: colour

Once your base coat is dry, it's time for your polish. Rest the hand being painted and the elbow of the other arm on a steady surface then try to apply your nail colour in just three brush strokes. When dry, apply a second coat if you need to. Remember, two thin coats are better than one gloopy layer!

Top Tip...

Don't pick or peel your nail colour off — it'll damage the nail beneath and leave rough patches... not nice!

Style Secret...

Apply one coat, allow to dry then always paint on another — the colour will be even more intense!

step 4: coat

Make sure your polish is well and truly dry then seal your work with a clear top coat. It'll add extra shine as well as keeping your colour for longer. Finished!

Style Secret...

Try a twist on the regular French manicure... paint your nails in a bright shade then add a neon colour for tips!

Top Tip...

Don't trim your cuticles! They're there to help protect your nails so cutting them can lead to infections. Gross!

step 5: treat

Finish your manicure with a super softening hand treatment. Sort rough 'n' ragged cuticles by massaging in a cuticle oil then gently push them back with an orange stick. Rub a hand cream into your hands before bed and let it work its magic whilst you get your beauty sleep! Easy.

manicure
must-haves...

- Emery Boards
- Buffer
- Base Coat
- Top Coat
- Cuticle Cream
- Orange Sticks
- Hand Cream

JEFF+MAGGIE

JEFF+MAGGIE

nails inc. 2. ridge remover
LONDON

johnson's
24hour moisture
hand cream

Feels soft even after
handwashing

Johnson&Johnson

Top
Coat
NAIL SPA CLUB
miss sporty

Cuticle
Cream
Nulon

super fast speed grow
base coat

miss
nail bar

nails inc.
LONDON

nail growth treatment
base coat
strengthens, toughens &
nourishes nails

nail polish heaven:
shout *faves...*

Collection 2000

Barry M

Miss Sporty

MAC

Rimmel

O.P.I

how to...
Fill Your *Free Time!*

Is it time for a new hobby?

Money is important to you — start

y → **You'd love to work on *Shout!***

n → **You regularly watch the news**

n → **You watch all the soaps**

y → **You keep a diary**

n → **P.E.'s one of your fave subjects**

n → **You worry about global warming**

y → **You ♥ trying out new looks**

y → **Cristiano's cuter than Zac!**

n → **You'd donate money to charity**

y

Go... *Creative!*

Why not try writing (a short story, an online blog... or even a song!), getting arty (get your bezzie or pet to pose for you!) or even experimenting with your clothes, make-up and hair to come up with a brand new you? Set your imagination free!

Go... *Sporty!*

Indoors or outdoors, there's loads to choose from, so have fun trying them all out! Netball, football, hockey, tennis, swimming, running... whether you fancy doing it as part of a team or going solo, we guarantee you won't be bored!

Go... *Voluntary!*

You're a caring, considerate girlie who hates to see anything suffer — whether it's animals, people or even the planet! — so being a volunteer's the hobby for you! Help at your local animal shelter or old people's home and make a difference!

perfect packing!

Don't even attempt to pack your case without reading this first!

THE RULES OF PACKING…

■ **Make a list of exactly what you need.**

■ Packing experts (oh yes, they exist!) recommend that you lay out all the clothes you think you'd like to take on hols on your bed… then half the pile, and half it again! Argh — sounds pretty drastic, but it's a fail-safe method — you really won't miss the stuff you leave behind!

■ **Remember — heavy stuff goes in the bottom of your case, so shoes, jeans, coats and towels should all be packed first to stop everything else being squashed by them!**

■ Pack shoes in plastic bags so that dirt and dust from the soles doesn't spoil your clothes.

■ **Rolling clothes rather than folding them helps to stop creases and lets you fit more stuff into your case!**

■ Fill gaps around the sides of your suitcase, in between clothes and inside your shoes with socks, bras, knickers, bikinis and tiny tops.

■ **Make sure that all the lids on toiletries are securely fastened — there's nothing worse than getting to your destination and finding your shampoo all over everything! Sellotaping the lids in place can help, and it's a good idea to store everything inside plastic bags to minimise damage if the worst does happen!**

■ Edit your make-up bag and include some multi-purpose products to save space!

WHAT A CARRY-ON!

Don't forget your all-important hand luggage! It's a good idea to use your beach bag or shopper as hand luggage — that way you're taking a bag that you will actually use on holiday!

■ Pack a spare pair of knickers, a clean top and any essential or valuable items like medication, phone, charger and camera in your hand luggage — that way, if your bag goes missing, it won't be the world's biggest disaster! And it goes without saying, passport, travel tickets and money go in there, too!

■ Remember that airlines have strict restrictions on carrying liquids on-board. Check the guidelines online before you fly, but as a rule, bottles must be no larger than 100ml, and you shouldn't bring more than a litre of liquids in total. Hurrah — an excuse to buy all those cute little travel-sized lotions and potions!

Don't forget to put something eye-catching on your case so that you can spot it amongst all the drab, boring cases at the baggage carousel! And write your name, home address and destination address on a luggage tag so that if your bags go walkabout, they'll find their way back to you somehow!

TURN OVER FOR MORE TIPS!

95

THE ESSENTIALS:

(How much you take depends on how long you're going for...)

Sunglasses
Sun cream
Toiletries
Make-up
Bikini or swimmie
Jeans and tops for day and night
A dress and/or cute top and skirt
Shorts or mini
Flipflops
Camera
Mobile
Adaptor plug
Prescription medicines
Hat
First-aid kit and sewing kit
Undies
Comfy shoes
Tampons/pads
Contact lenses/glasses

AND THE STUFF EVERYONE FORGETS!:

(So write this at the top of your list and make sure you tick 'em all off!)

Phone charger
Toothbrush
PJs or nightie
Hairbrush
Deodorant
Passport!
Contact lens solution

happy packing!

how to...
talk your way out of trouble!

It's time for some damage limitation!

In a sticky situation? Done something a teensy bit bad and it's come back to haunt you? Mum and Dad breathing down your neck, demanding answers? Teachers tormenting you? Well, don't just squirm... know how to talk your way out of trouble...!

Be confident

Mumbling, shaking and crying don't spell 'not guilty'! Take a deep breath and be confident — even if you're dying inside! Make eye contact, speak clearly and stand up straight... you'll seem much more convincing!

Tell the truth

Honesty really is the best policy! We know, we know, it can be hard to come out and admit the gory details of what you've done, but making things up or lying about the facts will actually be more harmful in the long run — liars almost always get found out!

Don't make excuses

No ifs, no buts — unless you have a really solid excuse, there's no point trying to make excuses — admit defeat! Lame excuses just make you look stupid!

Don't get angry

If you have done something wrong, then whoever's blaming you probably has good reason to be angry with you — but you're only angry with yourself for getting found out and for doing whatever it is in the first place! It's a bad idea to get angry — it won't do you any favours and you'll just be getting yourself into deeper trouble!

Admit when you're wrong

Everyone appreciates it when you can stand up and say, "I was wrong"... it takes guts (because really, who likes being wrong?!), but it's worth it, we promise.

Don't blame someone else...

Unless it really is their fault, of course! There's nothing worse than getting a mate or your brother and sister into trouble, just to get yourself out of it!

the
EX
factor!

Follow shout's top tips to help heal your broken heart…

Keep Your Distance!

Even if you've both decided to stay mates, you still need to take a complete break from seeing each other immediately after the break-up. This means avoiding the urge to call, text, e-mail or instant message him. Start by getting rid of his moby number and then scrub all evidence of his existence from your computer — that means deleting him from your Bebo, MySpace or Facebook profiles and your e-mail address book! It might seem a bit extreme, but it's really important that you avoid the temptation to get in touch with him for a while…

CHECK: ( )

Let It All Out!

It might feel like you're going through too many tissues but believe us, crying can be very healthy. Start by shutting your bedroom door behind you — then cry, scream, feel sorry for yourself and wallow in self-pity! We guarantee you that one day you'll wake up and you won't want to wallow any more, and each day after that you'll feel better and better! Soon, you'll have rediscovered your smile and you'll be ready to move on for good. And remember, if you don't let it all out in private, those feelings will just boil over and come out when you really don't want them to…

CHECK: ( )

Talk To Your Mates!

You've got to make sure that you keep communicating with your friends and family. Talking about what happened with your mates or your mum could help you move forward or just give you an outlet for your emotions. By surrounding yourself with people who love you, you'll always have a shoulder to cry on and they'll be able to help you deal with your feelings… Sometimes advice from a loved-one can go a long way.

CHECK: ( )

Remember His Flaws!

Don't get sucked into thinking that your ex was the absolute bee's knees. After all, it can be quite easy to well up thinking about his gorgeous blue eyes or how cute his dimples were when he smiled! What about all his bad points, though? It's important that you constantly remind yourself just how annoying, argumentative or insensitive he could be, and how boggin' his breath smelled from time-to-time! Remember his flaws and you'll be glad you broke up in no time…

CHECK:

Get Active!

Not only will it take your mind off things, but it's a scientific fact that exercise improves your mood! Doing something physical releases 'feel-good' chemicals in your body that make you feel happy — so why not go for a jog, join a dance class, head for hockey practise or just put on your favourite song and jump up and down on your bed?! Try to stick to healthy eating habits too — both of these promote positive thoughts and feelings!

CHECK:

Learn To Let Go!

Getting over your ex-boyfriend is going to be impossible if you're constantly thinking about what it would be like if you could get back together with him. You've just got to accept that you're single now and the best way to do that is to get rid of all the things that remind you of him. Chuck out any photos you have, get rid of little mementoes that you've collected and throw away all the presents he gave you. (Or if they're really good, just hide them for a while in the hope that you'll forget who gave them to you!) If you don't, it'll take much longer for you to stop feeling miserable…

CHECK:

Turn On The Style!

Whether you're off to a party, going shopping or just popping round to a mate's house, make sure you look totally gorgeous and glam. Slick on some eyeliner and lipgloss, put on a really cool outfit — and strut your stuff! You'll instantly feel much more confident about yourself and you never know whose eye you might catch!

CHECK: ▭

Don't Ponder The Past!

A lot of break-ups don't have one particular cause. They tend to happen when two people have been growing apart for a while and just don't feel the same way about each other any more. It's important not to keep obsessing about what went wrong! That isn't to say you shouldn't think about what you could have done differently in the relationship, but it isn't helpful to continually dwell on the past. Instead, start living in the moment and look towards the future — when the timing's right, you'll find a boyfriend who's a much better match than the last one. Who knows when you might bump into that special someone?!

CHECK: ▭

Treat Yourself!

Here's the good news — a break-up is the perfect excuse to indulge in the finer things in life! Why not hit the shops and pick up some pampering beauty products like a face mask, new nail polish and a big bottle of bubble bath? Then head home, run yourself a warm bath and try out everything you bought — we promise it'll make you feel completely refreshed. After all that, get your friends over and have a girlie night in watching a chick flick and munching on pizza and loads of sweet treats! Perfect!

CHECK: ▭

sun-kissed skin MADE SIMPLE!

Calling all golden girls… here's your guide to summer skin any time of the year!

STEP 1: Scrub Up

Dead skin cells that build up on your bod can make you look washed out and can make skin uneven, causing fake tan to end up patchy and streaky! No good for golden goddesses, so tackle dull skin by wakening it up with a body scrub, to help you prepare for your tanning experience!

TAN TIP: Pay close attention to your elbows, knees and shins cos the skin there tends to be extra dry, so polish them up to make sure they're silky smooth!

STEP 2: Softly, Softly...

Before you even think about applying fake tan, get your skin soft by using a moisturiser and, as with exfoliating, make sure to target the dry areas of your body. Look out for moisturisers specifically designed to prepare skin for tanning (hint — we love St Tropez Body Moisturiser, £12.00).

TAN TIP: Try to find a moisturiser that's not too heavy and let it dry into your skin before applying fake tan.

TURN OVER FOR MORE TIPS!

STEP 3: Tan!

Fake Bake tanning expert Lisa Fulton tells *Shout*, "Applying too much tanning product is a recipe for disaster! Only a certain amount of product can be absorbed during one application — the excess will simply rub off and result in an uneven tan." Follow her advice to get a gorgeous, even colour and try these tips for bronzing different areas of your body…

Face/Neck

Put the first dab of colour on your cheeks and work your way out, blending well under your neck and at the hairline. If you have blonde hair, watch you don't get any on your locks! Don't forget to wash your hands before and after application, especially if you're not wearing gloves.

Legs

Start with your lower legs, working your way from the ankles towards your knees and go lightly over your knees to avoid patchy colour, as they are often dry. Continue up your thighs and use whatever's left on your hands to go over your feet.

Back

Get help from your mum or a friend — don't attempt this area by yourself!

Arms

The same idea as your legs here — go lightly over elbows and remember to rinse hands afterwards to avoid yellow/orange stains between your fingers and on your palms! Look in a mirror to make sure you've covered the underside of your arms thoroughly — pale patches are not a good look!

Finishing Touches For Flawless Fake Tan…

Keep your tan looking the best it can by regularly moisturising every day — this works especially well just after a shower. Pat yourself down with a towel (rub too hard and your tan will end up on the towel!) and, whilst your skin is still damp, rub in loads of moisturiser! When you're in the shower, look for any areas that are fading and, if they're starting to look patchy, blitz them with a body scrub! You can always touch up when you're out of the shower and moisturised again!

Best if you want a deep tan...
Fake Bake

Best for a beachy glow...
Rimmel Sunshimmer

Best for glowy skin...
Garnier Ambre Solaire

fake tan faves

Best for A-list status...
St Tropez

Best for beginners...
Boots 17

All products available at time of press.

how to...

Find A *Hot New* Hairstyle...
Now!

Simply cut your face out of a photo and pop it in the spaces shown... Do you suit that style?

Before you head to the hairdresser, try the latest looks without the fear factor!

1.

2.

3.

4.

5.

1. *Long dark locks?*
2. *Caramel curls...*
3. *Tousled tresses*
4. *Up 'do?*
5. *Neat 'n' trendy curls...*

6. Volume and cool braiding...
7. Messy chic
8. Big impact curls
9. Sophisticated bunches
10. Side-pony style

6.

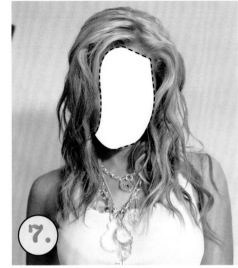

7.

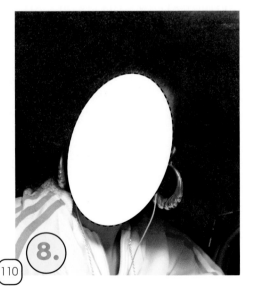

8.

9.

10.

11.

12.

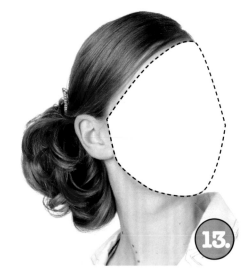

13.

14.

15.

11. *Pony with a twist…*
12. *Sleek, chic style*
13. *Funky bun*
14. *Mussed up 'n' trendy*
15. *Fluffed up bunches*

16. *Extra shiny bob...*
17. *Smooth 'n' straight*
18. *Try a wavy look...*
19. *What about choppy layers?*
20. *Pretty plait — cute!*

16.

17.

18.

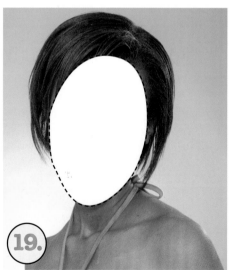

19.

20.

21.

22.

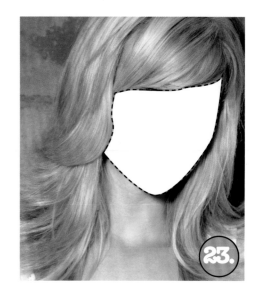

23.

24.

25.

21. *Candy floss cut...*
22. *Accessorise with cute clips*
23. *Blonde ambition*
24. *Seaside curls = sexy*
25. *This fringe suits long faces...*

EXAMS
Stressing You Out?!

Which of our three stress-busters is the one for you?!...

start

Are you normally the centre of attention?

y → Are your mates stressed out too?

n → Are you a girlie girl?

Are your mates stressed out too?
- **y** → Do you see enough of your mates?
- **n** → Do you work well in a group?

Do you work well in a group?
- **y** → Do you see enough of your mates?
- **n** → Do your mates come to you for advice?

Do you see enough of your mates?
- **y** →
- **n** → Are you a shy person?

Do your mates come to you for advice?
- **y** → Do you get enough time on your own?
- **n** →

Are you a girlie girl?
- **y** →
- **n** → Do you get angry for no reason?

Do you get angry for no reason?
- **n** →
- **y** → Do you struggle to sleep at night?

Are you a shy person?
- **n** → BOWLING

Do you get enough time on your own?
- **y** → Are you a shy person?
- **n** → BATH

Do you struggle to sleep at night?
- **y** → BATH
- **n** → BOXERCISE

BOWLING
We think the best thing you can do is spend some time with your friends trying out something new. You're all stressed out and could do with having fun — why not try ten-pin bowling? It's a brilliant laugh and there are always hot blokes around!

114

BATH
You need some time just for yourself, so why not have the most relaxing bath ever?! Shut yourself off from the world and totally indulge yourself with candles, bubble bath or anything else that smells delicious! You'll soon forget your exam worries!

BOXERCISE
Why not take yourself along to a boxercise class?! Loads of stars are big fans of this top stress-buster and, don't worry, you'll only be taking your tension out on a punch bag — and you'll end up with a fab, toned body and a stress-free head!

how to...
Understand
Your
Parents

Think they're just yelling at you? Think again...

Parents get annoyed...

... when you don't talk to them...

because they don't know what's going on in your life! If you just ignore them until you need a lift somewhere, they'll be less likely to help. Chat to them about your mates and homework and they'll be more willing to pull favours for you, we promise! Hey, if it means not having to walk to school when it's raining then it must be worth it...

... when they don't know who your mates are...

because they care about you! If they know all your mates are lovely (which they are, so no problem) then they won't mind you going to massive sleepovers and the like — because they know you won't be running wild in the streets at 4am! Letting them meet your mates just makes your life a little easier!

... when you wear a teeny tiny skirt/cake on loads of make-up/spend AGES on the net...

again it's that old chestnut — because they care! Basically, they don't want you to grow up too fast or end up in a dodgy situation. This may sound a bit rubbish, but on the flip side, it might just mean that your mum will still treat you to new clothes occasionally! That's instead of you being all grown up and independent, and er... having to pay for them yourself!

... when you don't do your homework...

because they want you to do well! It's not just because they like to nag at you, honest! And if they can see you're making an effort during the week then they're much more likely to let you lounge around at the weekend, hassle-free! Sounds good to us...

Celebs look fab 24/7, so why not steal their hot fashion?…

Brantano

New Look

Red Herring at Debenhams

Miso at Republic

For the ultimate red carpet style, you can't go wrong with an LBD. Team it with cute heels and some over-the-top bling and you'll be the talk of the party!

Red Carpet Glam *Hilary Duff*

Evie at Peacocks

Crafted at Republic

Accessorize

New Look

www.dollydagger.co.uk

Fun 'N' Funky *Rihanna*

Keep your look fun by teaming jeans with a girlie top. To dress up your look, try adding bold jewellery and daring make-up.

119

Shoe Express

H&M

Primark

Miso at Republic

Dorothy Perkins

Red Herring at Debenhams

Biker Chick *Vanessa Hudgens*

A dressy top, heels and skinny jeans are the ultimate style combo, but why not pop on a biker jacket to give your pretty look a rock edge?

Generation 915
at New Look

Levi's

Primark

Red Herring at
Debenhams

Claire's

Jane
Norman

High Street Chic *Lily Allen*

Shopping calls for simple yet elegant style. Who wants to remove a million pieces of clothing when there are so many shops to get around?! A plain jacket, jeans and pumps will keep you looking smart without the fuss!

121

Quiz

Freedom at
Topshop

Accessorize

Freedom at
Topshop

Faith

Sometimes a girl just can't be sparkly
enough! Take a leaf out of B's book and
fearlessly load on the glitz and glamour
— and don't forget the big hair!

Queen Of Bling *Beyoncé*

Topshop

Accessorize

Crafted at Republic

Peacocks

Office

Soul Cal at Republic

Laid Back Cool *Fearne Cotton*

When you feel like chilling out, don't put your sloppy joes on — keep your cool in a funky dress and shirt. Try mis-matching some of your items for instant indie style.

Claire's

Primark

Faith

www.boohoo.com

www.boohoo.com

Jane Norman

A blazer can totally transform your outfit from plain to smart in seconds! Adding dashes of colour will brighten up your look, and if you're suffering from a bad hair day — pop on a smart cap and step out in style!

Smarty Pants *Christina Aguilera*

New Look

La Senza

QS

Accessorize

H&M

H&M

High Fashion *Ashley Olsen*

Okay, getting that 'stylish-but-I'm-not-trying-to-be' look is pretty difficult to achieve, so why not try some Olsen-style experimenting? Simple items like black jeans and a checked shirt can be worn in a million ways. Sunnies and an oversized bag will make you look like an A-lister, guaranteed!

All products available at time of press.

how to...
make the *perfect*
ice cream
sundae!

Want to know the secrets to a spectacular sundae? All will be revealed...

YOU'LL NEED:

● A serving dish that's big enough to hold plenty of ice cream, drizzled syrup and added toppings!

● A special spoon with a long handle that's ideal for scooping everything out!

The Sundae

● Pick a flavour of ice cream. Choose a plain rather than an overpowering flavour as you're going to be adding lots of other ingredients. The ice cream should be the background flavour to all the additions! Popular ice cream sundae flavours are vanilla, chocolate and strawberry.

● Scoop out three portions of ice cream and place in the sundae dish.

The Toppings

● Drizzle some chocolate sauce or any other flavoured syrup over each scoop of ice cream. Make sure the syrup has been stored in the fridge as this thickens its consistency. Try zig-zagging the syrup over the ice cream and even adding different syrups for a taste sensation!

Finally, add sprinkles, whipped cream, fruit or anything you fancy like pieces of your favourite choccy bar, Smarties or M&Ms, and finish off the sundae with some whipped cream.

Turn over to find more tasty toppings!

Chocolate Sundae: Classic vanilla ice cream, choc sauce and whipped cream topped off with a cherry make this the all-time fave feast!

Fudge Sundae: Hot fudge sauce and walnuts make this an irresistible treat!

Knickerbocker Glory: This old-fashioned sundae is still going strong. Add jelly and pieces of fruit to ice cream and serve in a posh glass!

Strawberry Sundae: Mix pieces of fruit with strawberry and vanilla ice cream for a top dessert, and finish off with a wafer!

make the most of *your mates!*

Hanging with your friends is never boring!

What? Stay Over!

● *Shout* readers love nothing better than a girlie sleepover! Get a few of your closest mates together and arrange a night at someone's house (get them to check with their parents first, of course!). Stock up on things like pizza, crisps and pop (why not suggest everyone brings one thing?), hire a few of the latest DVDs, look out your fave CDs… and get ready to party!

How?

● The best thing about sleepovers is that you've got all night so there's loads of time to have fun! You can chat about lads, have a clothes swap, try out different hair and make-up looks or come up with new dances for your fave tunes, or you can just throw on your PJs and chill out watching films and eating. What's not to like?!

What To Talk About:

● Family, school, lads, fashion, celebs… anything!

What Not To Do:

● Fall asleep! Not only will you miss out on all the fun, your mates might decide to play a practical joke on you…
● Get bitchy! We all love a good gossip, but make sure it stays just that — you wouldn't like it if you knew other people were saying horrible things about you, would you?!

What? Watch A Film!

● Go to see a hot new movie at the cinema. After all, it's so much better seeing your crush on the huge screen!

How?

● Round up some mates who want to see it too and arrange a time that suits everyone. You can either all meet in the entrance hall or perhaps one of your parents can give you a lift.
● Don't forget your muchies! Cinema food can be pretty expensive so, if it's just crisps and sweets you normally buy, it's much cheaper to bring your own. If you can't go to the pictures without getting a hot dog or popcorn, though, make sure you leave enough time to get these before the film starts.

What To Talk About:

● Erm… nothing! You're there to watch a film, remember?!

What Not To Do:

● Talk! It's okay to chat during the trailers but it's really annoying when someone near you whispers and giggles when you're trying to watch a film — so make sure this person isn't you or your mates! You could even risk being chucked out before Zac Efron's even sung his first song — disaster!
● Chuck popcorn or sweets around. Again, you could end up being thrown out… or even banned!

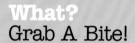

What?
Hit The High Street!

● You've seen the hot new trends in *Shout*, so now's the time to try them out!

How?

● Saturdays are definitely best for shopping! You've got the whole day to spend trying stuff on, and you can stop off for snacks or a drink whenever you want!
● Make sure you've got comfy shoes on so you don't end up with aching tootsies, and clothes that are pretty easy to get in and out of — less time struggling with your buttons/zips/belts means more time to try on lots of clothes!
● Take more than one item into the changing room at a time. Get your mate(s) to do the same then hit the changing rooms together.

What To Talk About:

● How great you both look! You'll have a real laugh showing each other your outfits and mixing and matching pieces — you might come up with a fab new style!

What Not To Do:

● Be honest, but in a nice way. If your mate looks awful in an outfit, don't tell her how bad she looks! Instead, suggest she tries on something else that you know will suit her better and then tell her how fab she looks in it.

What?
Grab A Bite!

● Save up a bit of cash and go out for pizza with your friends.

How?

● Going when there's an 'all you can eat' deal on means you'll get more for your money or, if there's enough of you, why not get a selection of toppings and share them between you all?

What To Talk About:

● Pretty much anything — as long as you can talk with your mouth full!

What Not To Do:

● Make too much noise! Yep, you're there to have a laugh but you don't want to be so loud that you annoy any other people there. After all, if you get kicked out, who's gonna finish your food?!
● Complain that one of your mates has eaten more than anyone else so should pay extra! Splitting the bill equally is much easier — you never know, it might be you who's the greedy guts the next time you're out!
● Spill food on yourself — mega cringe!

Liquid Liner – Step-By-Step!

Foolproof tricks to help you get 100% perfect peepers!

Step 1:

Sit in front of a well-lit mirror, and stabilise your liquid lining hand by propping your elbow on a desk or dressing table. Shaky hands = dodgy liner!

 HINT! If you're in a hurry, give liquid liner a miss — you'll need to give yourself time to get it perfect.

Step 2:

Begin your sophisticated look with eyeshadow first, liquid liner will go over the top of neutral colours easily.

 HINT! For a classic Hollywood look, go for a nude shadow and team with jet black liquid liner but for a brighter eye, bold purple or turquoise will suit everyone!

Step 3:

Start lining your upper lids by drawing a few dots (kind of a dot-to-dot for liquid liner!) just above your lashes. You'll find it easier to go back and join them together in one smooth step rather than trying to draw a line in one.

Look down your nose into a mirror for more accurate lining and less smudging! **HINT!**

Step 4:

When your liner is applied, keep your eyes half-closed for a minute to allow the colour to dry and prevent it smearing on to the rest of your lid.

HINT! Look out for make-up corrector pens — they'll clear up mistakes without taking off the rest of your make-up!

Step 5:

Finish your liquid liner with a brown or black mascara to keep it classy or if you're feeling colour confident, opt for bright shades and prepare to sizzle!

HINT! Turn your eyeshadow into a liquid liner by dampening a thin eye or lip brush before applying.

Photography: Simon Taylor
Hair & Make-up: Bea Burton

Trendy

Claire's Cosmetics

Strong

Barry M

Subtle

Wet N Wild

Beyoncé-style

2True

Chic

M.A.C

Classy

No7

All products available at time of press.

how to...
Find A Celeb Hairstyle!

Suss out the star style for you!

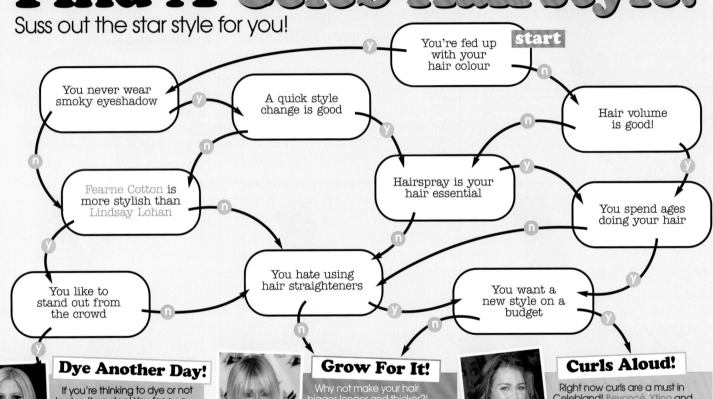

start — You're fed up with your hair colour

- y → You never wear smoky eyeshadow
  - y → A quick style change is good
  - n → Fearne Cotton is more stylish than Lindsay Lohan
    - y → You like to stand out from the crowd
      - y → **Dye Another Day!**
    - n → You hate using hair straighteners
- n → Hair volume is good!
  - n → Hairspray is your hair essential
  - y → You spend ages doing your hair
    - y → You want a new style on a budget
    - n → You hate using hair straighteners

A quick style change is good
- n → Fearne Cotton...
- y → Hairspray is your hair essential

Hairspray is your hair essential
- n → You hate using hair straighteners

You spend ages doing your hair
- n → You hate using hair straighteners
- y → You want a new style on a budget

You hate using hair straighteners
- n → **Grow For It!**
- y → You want a new style on a budget

You want a new style on a budget
- n → **Grow For It!**
- y → **Curls Aloud!**

Dye Another Day!

If you're thinking to dye or not to dye, then stop! You fancy a change and, like **Avril Lavigne**, you don't like to follow the crowd. But remember, if you're looking for a specific colour and want the job done right, go to a professional!

136

Grow For It!

Why not make your hair bigger, longer and thicker?! Like **Paris**, you can add instant lengthy tresses and look glam at the same time. Once applied, they're easy to care for, so don't let **Britney**'s minging clip-in extensions put you off!

Curls Aloud!

Right now curls are a must in Celebland! Beyoncé, Xtina and Miley Cyrus are among those who have been working their waves, ringlets and twists lately and it's about time you joined them. It'll be high on time but low on cost, and most certainly worth it!

Sleep Easy!

Here's how to have a
great night's sleep...

● Sip a hot drink — and we don't mean coffee! Try a hot chocolate, a warm milk or a special herbal tea designed to help you drift off. Zzzzzzzz…

● Having a warm bath can help you to unwind and lets your body and mind relax before bed. Try adding some specially-formulated bedtime bubble bath for the ultimate night-time indulgence…

● *If you still can't sleep, don't lie in bed tossing and turning. Get up and do something, like reading or even tidying out a drawer or organising your clothes — and once you feel tired, hop straight back into bed!*

● *If you live on a busy road and traffic noise keeps you awake at night, invest in some earplugs! They won't block out all the noise, but they will provide a bit of relief!*

● Avoid eating too much before bed. Snacking before bed could lead to a disturbed night's sleep, because your body will be busy digesting food rather than concentrating on sleep!

● **An eyemask can help you drift off — and stops you being rudely awakened by those early morning rays!**

● Make your bedroom a haven of tranquillity and peace. Keep it as tidy as possible (easier said than done, we know!) and spray a soothing lavender spray in the air to help calm and relax you.

● *Find your perfect pillow! Don't put up with whatever's going spare around the house — everyone likes something different, so take time to discover your fave!*

● Turn off all electrical appliances like computers, TVs and DVD recorders and digiboxes — they all make an annoying noise, and when you're having a hard time sleeping, it can seem 100% louder!

sweet dreams!

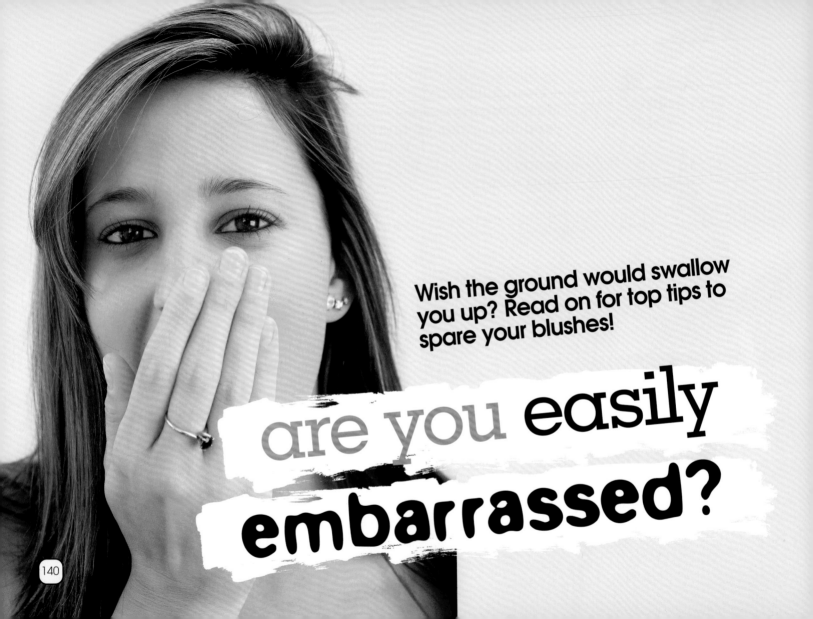

Wish the ground would swallow you up? Read on for top tips to spare your blushes!

are you easily embarrassed?

Let's face it, we've all been embarrassed at some point in our lives and even top celebs own up to their red-face situations... but what can you do to get over an embarrassing moment? Stop crying and try these...

10 If your EM happens in the school corridor or outside the loos, for example, then get away from the scene as soon as possible! The quicker you go somewhere else the sooner everyone staring will forget what happened!

9 Laugh at yourself! Yes, we know it sounds like the last thing you'd want to do... but if other people see you laughing they'll feel like they can laugh at you too and it'll break the ice. Rather than being the joke you'll become part of the joke!

8 Who's next?! Remember that although you're in the spotlight just now it'll be someone else before long. Yes, you're embarrassed now but it'll be someone else's turn next!

Turn over for more!

6 Talk it over! If you're worried that people will never forget what's happened then maybe you should talk about it with someone responsible, like an older sister, your parents or even a teacher. We bet it's not as bad as you think it is and a little reassurance goes a long way!

5 Take your mind off things... do something like visiting the cinema or going shopping with your bezzies! You'll end up having so much fun that you'll forget what happened... and even if you don't, you'll have had so much fun you won't be bothered anymore!

7 Learn from your mistakes. If your EM involved a boy (your super-hot crush we're guessing) then ask yourself where you went wrong! Talk to him on his own the next time or plan what you're going to say. Whatever the EM, learn from it!

4 Forget about it! We know this is easier said that done… but make a conscious effort not to dwell on what's happened. Set yourself a limit if you have to… for example, after 12pm you will refuse to think about being embarrassed. This really works!

3 Ask your mates to help you. If you've embarrassed yourself in front of the 'cool' crowd then ask your mates to back you up! Let them help you show the world that you're not bothered about what happened… you're all too busy having fun to care!

2 Pick up a copy of your favourite magazine, *Shout*… and head straight for our *Embarrassing Moments* pages. After laughing at our readers' mad cringes you'll soon realise yours wasn't anywhere near as bad as you first thought — why not send yours in as well and you could win £20 in the process!

1 Smile! Smile! Smile! That's right… it's that simple. The single best thing you can do to get over your embarrassing moment is to smile. Nothing puts you and other people in a better mood than a gleaming, big smile. If you can show that you're not bothered by what's happened then everyone else will soon begin to ask themselves if it's worth laughing about.

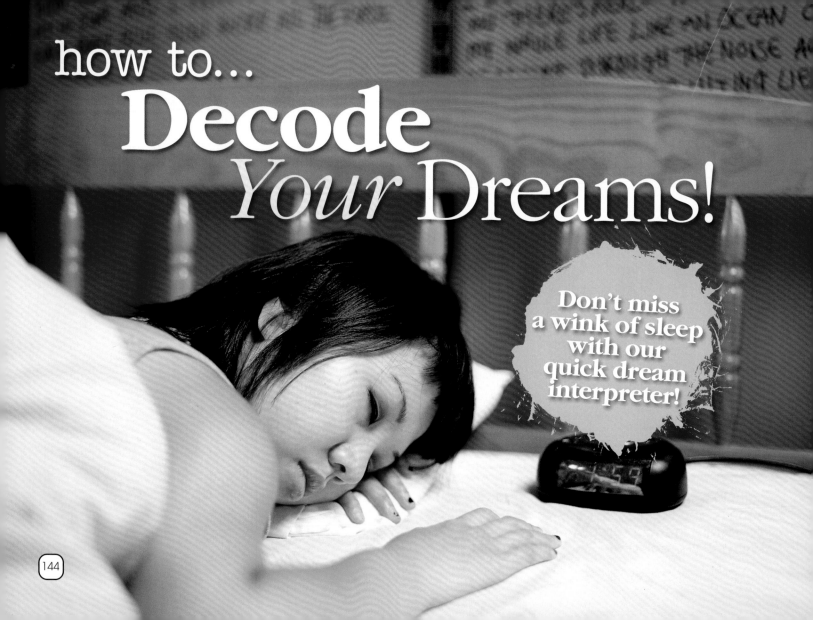

how to...
Decode
Your Dreams!

Don't miss a wink of sleep with our quick dream interpreter!

Flying

There are two reasons for flying in dreams:

1. You have a strong desire to travel.
2. You need to escape a dangerous situation.

Check out the most common dreams and discover what you really think and feel!

Water

Water is the symbol of new life, but the amount of water is important to what the dream represents:

● Travelling on calm water reflects that you are happy with your life and aren't afraid of change.

● Uncontrolled water like rapids and storms show that you feel uncomfortable with a change in your life.

Kissing

Kissing in a dream is a wish-fulfilment, not necessarily to be kissed, but to feel loved. You want to feel cared for, or you want to care for other people. But if you're dreaming of kissing your crush, it probably does mean you want to kiss him! Like we needed to tell you that!

Nudity

It's really common to dream about being naked in unusual places. And it's no surprise that it shows you feel vulnerable. Look at where you're naked — this might be the place where you feel least secure.

Money

Money represents power and control. Your role with the money is the most important part of the dream...

- **Gaining money:** The person you get the money from gives you emotional support.
- **Giving money:** You want to help people, not necessarily financially though.
- **Losing money:** You have a lack of self-control.

Falling

Falling is an indication of insecurity, instability and anxiety. You might feel overwhelmed by a situation in your waking life. It's also a sign of failure or feeling inferior — particularly if you've failed an exam, broken up, or your home life is unstable.

Losing Someone/ Something

Dreams about losing the things you love are important as the things we value most are an extension of ourselves, and it can mean that we're afraid of losing who we really are.

- **Losing an object:** You're scared you forget the past.
- **Losing a person:** You're questioning your commitment to that relationship.

Colour

It's possible to dream completely in colour. These colours represent emotions…

Blue: Tranquility or depression.
Black: Power or death.
Green: Wealth or envy.
Red: Passion or danger.
White: Purity or emptiness.
Yellow: Friendship or illness.
Purple: Growth or injury.

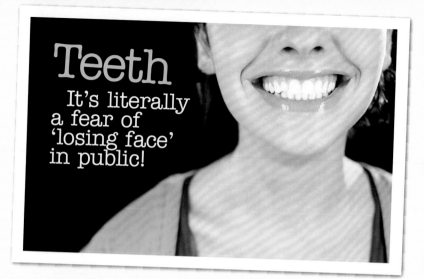

Teeth

It's literally a fear of 'losing face' in public!

Running

Running is usually a bad omen.

● Running from danger and escaping it shows that you are emotionally drained from a past situation.

● Running from danger and stumbling, never escaping the fear, relates to a real-life situation where you feel pressure.

Travel

You're undergoing changes in your life and the type vehicle you're travelling in can tell you a lot about your emotions.

● **Car:** If you're driving it shows that you're full of ambition and responsibility, but being a passenger suggests that you're happy to let other people take charge.

● **Train:** You're reaching a goal in your life at a fast pace, and there's no way for you to turn back.

● **Aeroplane:** You want to do bigger and better things. You crave adventure.

● **Boat:** Water = emotions. Therefore travelling on water means you're going through an emotional change and the type of water represents how strong your feelings are.

EXPRESS

De-stress!

Exams, family, friends… ever feel like life's getting on top of you? Here's how to chill out…

GET ORGANISED!

Sometimes we make stress for ourselves! If you're always running late in the morning, you'll arrive at school in a fluster… and you'll probably be in the bad books with your teachers, too!

Make an effort to streamline your morning routine — that means laying out your school clothes the night before, getting everything together that you might need the next day — P.E. kit, any permission forms that need to be signed by your parents, your packed lunch — oh, and set your alarm a bit earlier, too!

If your problem is never being able to find anything, there's only one solution… it's time to blitz that bedroom! Boring, we know, but you'll find that knowing where everything is makes life 100% easier! You might even rediscover some clothes you'd forgotten you had…

Blitz that bedroom!

IT'S GOOD TO TALK…

Share your worries.

Put things in perspective by discussing your worries with a mate or someone in your family. Bottling things up can make you feel even worse, and sometimes we build problems up in our heads until they seem much worse than they really are. Someone else's point of view can help you make a plan of action and see things as they really are!

ASK FOR HELP

When life's getting on top of you and you're feeling really stressed, don't go it alone! Think about who can help you, and ask for help! It could be something as simple as your dad helping you recite your French verb tables, your mate organising a night out instead of you, or your brother doing a couple of your chores for you (yep, we know you'll have to pay him back for that one in the future!)… every little helps!

Don't go it alone!

AND… RELAX!

If all else fails, take a deep breath and make some time for yourself! If you're up to your eyeballs in textbooks it can be hard to take a break, but you need it! Regular breaks help stop tiredness and allow your brain to absorb the facts you've just been reading.

Or if your family or friends are stressing you out, indulge yourself in some 'me' time — we're imagining baths, face masks, bubbles and hot chocolate! Just stepping away from a situation can help you to unwind and make sense of it. Everything seems better after a bath!

Take a deep breath.

how to...
wear **Bright** & **Bold** clothes!

Our colour guide will help you to be a style sensation in no time!

Skin Tone SUSSED!

Wearing the right colour can be tricky — you don't want to look pale and washed out or like a traffic light. So first thing's first — get your skin tone sussed! Find the best one to match yours and you're on your way to becoming a colourful cutie!

Kirsten Dunst

Bright Babe

Hair: Blonde or brown.
Eyes: Green or blue.
Skin: Pale with rosy cheeks.
Shade Sensation... Go for fresh, zesty colours like yellow, pink, green, turquoise, blue and coral!
Colour Catastrophe... Steer clear of dark or contrasting colours like black and white.

Lindsay Lohan

Vanessa Hudgens

Mischa Barton

Spice Girl

Hair: Red, blonde and brown.
Eyes: Hazel, green or brown.
Skin: Pale, burns easily and may have freckles.
Shade Sensation… You'll look lush in spicy colours like orange, gold and red.
Colour Catastrophe… Pink might clash with your hair…

Dark & Mysterious

Hair: Dark.
Eyes: Hazel, green or brown.
Skin: African, Asian, olive.
Shade Sensation… You lucky thing! You suit most colours, especially neon and metallic…
Colour Catastrophe… Stay away from pastels as they'll make you look drained…

Blue Belle

Hair: Blonde or brown.
Eyes: Grey-ish.
Skin: Pale.
Shade Sensation… You look better than anyone else in blue. And why not check out pink, purple and pale yellow while you're at it?
Colour Catastrophe… Drastic colours like orange and black should be avoided!

Wrangler

COMFORT
AND
STYLE

Roxy

Matalan

WE ❤
THIS!

Yellow

Tammy at BHS

Faith

COLOURFUL
TOOTSIES

Matalan

■ Summer just wouldn't be the same without yellow! It's a cute colour that will suit most skin tones and it can really give your outfit a refreshing twist.
■ Get yourself a pretty yellow top or a gorge bag for instant summer style!

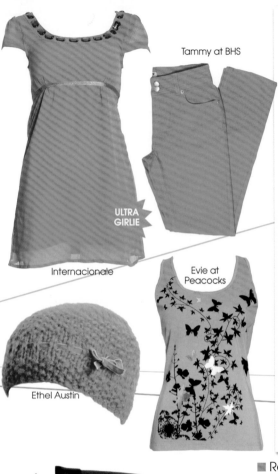

Tammy at BHS

ULTRA GIRLIE

Internacionale

Ethel Austin

Evie at Peacocks

Pink

Tammy at BHS

New Look

Tammy at BHS

ADD GLITTER!

Claire's

■ Release your inner princess by wearing pretty pink!
■ Whether you're meeting your gal pals for a spot of power shopping, or just hanging out at McDonald's, you're bound to look cute in pink!
■ But don't overdo it — too much pink can make you look more Barbie than babe! Combine it with denim, white or yellow to tone it down and remember to flutter your eyelashes for the ultimate girlie accessory!

Primark

Roxy

Reebok

STYLISH
SNEAKERS

Internacionale

Keds

Nike

NIKE
AIR

SPORTY
GALS TAKE
NOTE!

Orange

■ Orange has got wow factor, that's for sure! You won't
go unnoticed wearing this lush shade…
■ Orange looks fab during most seasons of the year. It gives a
happy, sunny feel in spring and summer, and looks perfect with
natural, autumn shades, so you'll get a lot of wear out of it!

Cherokee at Tesco

CUTE POCKETS!

Primark

H&M

Primark

Matalan

HOT HEAD Primark

Tammy at BHS

Office

Blue

BEAUTIFUL BELT

New Look

■ Blue isn't just for boys — it's for looking totally hot!
■ Whether you go for pretty pale blue for a softer look, or electric blue for a fun-loving approach, you're sure to look lush.
■ Blue and black go together well for a classy night-time look. Or pair it with white for that cool nautical feel during the day.

H&M

Barratts

New Look

FLATTERS ALL SHAPES

www.boohoo.com

Billabong

MIX 'N' MATCH GREEN TONES

NATURAL SHADES

O'Neill

Vans

Green

■ Go green and chill out! It's a natural colour that can be as bright or as neutral as you like. Different shades of green look good together as well, so there's no problem with clashing colours!

■ Green's quite understated, so there's nothing to fear when you wear it!

■ A pair of green jeans can really transform your look without going over the top. It's definitely one of the easiest colours to wear, and one of our faves!

Rocket Dog

WINTER ESSENTIAL

Jane Norman

ADD HEELS FOR GLAM

Bay Trading

Look at Freemans

TREAT YOUR FEET

Purple

Shoe Express

Primark

CUTE GOLD DETAIL

H&M

adidas

H&M

■ Look sleek and glamorous in pretty purple!
■ Purple screams A-list celeb so make sure you add plenty of jewels — gold looks fab! It's been the hot colour on the catwalk and it looks like it's going nowhere, so stock up on some purple goodies for your wardrobe!

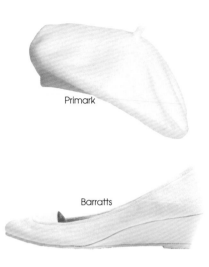

Primark

Barratts

Primark

White

HOT MUST-HAVE

Primark

Evie at Peacocks

GLAM UP WITH BLING!

■ Okay, so it's technically not a colour, but we thought it deserved a mention!

■ Don't underestimate how good white can look! In summer it'll keep you looking crisp, fresh and cool. And in winter, it'll give your look a nice, wintry feel. Silver looks stunning paired with white as they're both icy shades, and denim and white are an all-time classic colour combo!

ULTIMATE SUMMER STYLE

Primark

Primark

Brantano

Golddigga

LAID BACK COOL

H&M

New Look

PRETTY PATENT

Tammy at BHS

GLAM!

H&M

Primark

Diva at Miss Selfridge

Red

■ Red screams 'glamour'... why else is it called the red carpet?! So perfect your pout and get ready to strut in red...

■ The key to wearing red is to be super-confident. It's one of the brightest colours, so you'll get a lot of attention. There's no point in trying to blend into the background if your outfit screams 'look at me'!

■ If you're scared to go for all-out red, then add bold splashes of it into your look. A red bag or jewellery will accentuate your outfit and grab attention where it's wanted!

All products available at time of press.

160

how do you
Rate As A Mate?

Are you the best friend ever? Find out…

start

Other people's problems are boring
— no → **You'd let a mate borrow your clothes**
— yes → **You're the agony aunt of your group!**

Other people's problems are boring — yes → **You're always interrupting people**

You'd let a mate borrow your clothes — yes → **You're the agony aunt of your group!**
You'd let a mate borrow your clothes — no → **You've got lots of hobbies**

You're the agony aunt of your group! — no → **You're terrible at replying to texts**
You're the agony aunt of your group! — yes → **You never ever lose your temper**

You're always interrupting people — no → **You've got lots of hobbies**
You're always interrupting people — yes → **You're a bit of an attention-seeker!**

You've got lots of hobbies — no → **You're terrible at replying to texts**
You've got lots of hobbies — yes → **Your mates' secrets are safe with you!**

You're terrible at replying to texts — no → **Your mates' secrets are safe with you!**
You're terrible at replying to texts — yes → **You'd cancel plans with pals for a lad**

You never ever lose your temper — no → **Your mates' secrets are safe with you!**
You never ever lose your temper — yes → **You'd cancel plans with pals for a lad**

You're a bit of an attention-seeker! — no → **Your mates' secrets are safe with you!**
You're a bit of an attention-seeker! — yes → *(You're so self-centred!)*

Your mates' secrets are safe with you! — no / yes →

You'd cancel plans with pals for a lad — yes / no →

You're *so* self-centred!

It's hard to be a great mate when your fave topic of conversation is YOU! Your mates love your personality and think you're fun to be with, but you need to try being less selfish! Learn to listen to what others are saying!

You're a part-time pal!

When you're around you can be a top mate, but all too often you're too busy to hang out with your friends. It's great being popular with lads and having hobbies — but remember how important it is to make time for your pals as well!

You're a fantastic friend!

You're as loyal, thoughtful and forgiving as friends come! Your mates always turn to you for advice and know they can count on you in a crisis! What happens when you need help, though? Make sure they're there for you too!

161

how to...
survive
a school trip!

Got any worries? Well don't fear, cos **shout's** here!

162

1 So you've got a long bus journey coming up and someone loud you don't want to listen to is going to be on it. Well, take your iPod and load it with some fab new tunes before you go. Sorted!

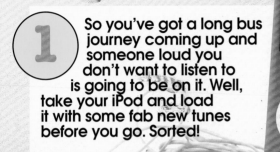

2 If you're going away for a few days then be prepared for all types of weather conditions. You don't want to look silly with shorts on while it's raining. Plus, the more clothes you take, the more choice you'll have!

3 Are you worried about not having enough spending money? Then do some extra chores at home before you go to earn some extra pocket money!

4 Keep make-up to a minimum: your school trip essentials are concealer, blush or bronzer, mascara (make it waterproof) and a spritz of your favourite perfume!

5 Make sure your mobile is fully charged. You don't want it dying on you when you go to text everyone back home about how good a time you're having!

Turn over for more!

6 Do you suffer from travel sickness? If so, avoid heavy meals before travelling. Alternatively, anti-sickness medicines are available from the chemist and these should be used according to the instructions.

7 If you're worried about getting your first period on the trip, never fear! Be prepared with a little 'period kit', including wrapped towels or tampons, tissues and a spare pair of knickers in case of emergencies! If you do start while you're away, there will be loads of teachers and mates to confide in and ask for advice.

If you've already started and you've worked out that your period is due while you're away, go armed with supplies. If swimming or watersports are involved, you won't be able to wear a pad while doing these. Don't despair, though — you can wear a tampon in water, so if you've never tried one before, why not give them a go on your next period?

No need to waste time worrying about periods — just go and have fun!

DON'T PANIC!

8 If you're not happy with a certain someone who may be going on the trip or think you may be a victim of bullying, then please let a teacher know before you go. The teacher can keep an eye on anything nasty happening or, better still, ban the bully!

9 You could be sitting next to your crush on the bus, or teamed up with him in a task. So, think up some topics of conversation before you go — you don't want to be left tongue-tied and red-faced!

10 Keep wipes handy! Not only will they remove make-up but you'll keep your hands clean wherever you are and whatever you're doing.

gentle cleansing MAKE-UP REMOVER WIPES
15 per
open here

11 Not happy with the sleeping arrangements? If this is really bothering you, then let a teacher know. However, remember that you'll be too busy sleeping to be bothered about who your roommates are!

12 If you're not looking forward to an activity, nobody will force you to do anything. There will be others in the same boat though, so why not just give everything a go and, who knows, you may enjoy it!

13 If you want to make bedtime more interesting then pop some sweets in your bag for a midnight feast! You'll be Little Miss Popular when you pull out a super-sized bag of something tasty!

14 Hair looking greasy? If you haven't been able to wash your hair or your style's suffering in hot conditions, pop it in a sleek ponytail or up 'do — hair that's not freshly washed will style more easily!

15 If you're going abroad then why not take a phrase book? You'll impress all your mates with the local lingo!

16 Take a copy of **shout** with you! Full of quizzes, true stories, fashion and beauty, embarrassing moments and all the latest celeb news — everyone will be regretting not taking their copy!

137

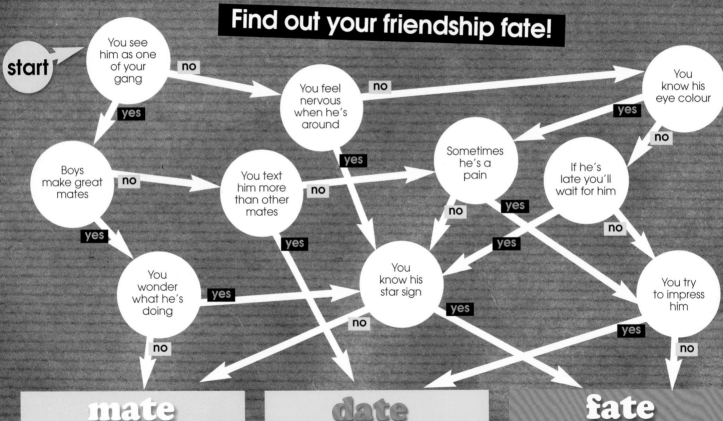

Is he a Mate or a Date?

Find out your friendship fate!

start → You see him as one of your gang — no → You feel nervous when he's around — no → You know his eye colour

You see him as one of your gang — yes → Boys make great mates

Boys make great mates — no → You text him more than other mates

Boys make great mates — yes → You wonder what he's doing

You feel nervous when he's around — yes → You know his star sign

You text him more than other mates — no → Sometimes he's a pain

You text him more than other mates — yes → (down)

You wonder what he's doing — yes → You know his star sign

You wonder what he's doing — no → **mate**

You know his eye colour — yes → If he's late you'll wait for him

You know his eye colour — no → You try to impress him

Sometimes he's a pain — no → You know his star sign

Sometimes he's a pain — yes → (down)

If he's late you'll wait for him — yes → Sometimes he's a pain

If he's late you'll wait for him — no → You try to impress him

You know his star sign — yes → (down)

You know his star sign — no → **date**

You try to impress him — yes → (down)

You try to impress him — no → **fate**

mate　**date**　**fate**

mate

He has his good points and you'd be lost without him but right now he's definitely more of a mate! You need to look elsewhere for date material!

date

Come on, you fancy him big time! Maybe you just need to admit to yourself once and for all that he's so much more of a date than a mate!

fate

Will you get together or stay good friends? No-one knows right now, not even you! Relax! Have fun and if it's fate then you're sure to date!

how to...
Make Your Lipgloss Work Harder!

Follow these quick tips for the perfect pout!

■ Be a softie!
Start by making sure your lips are super soft. If they feel dry or flaky, gently rub with a soft toothbrush to get rid of any dry skin.

■ Beauty Sleep!
While you snooze, your beauty products still work for you. Slick a layer of Vaseline on your lips every night before you go to bed and let it get to work while you catch some beauty sleep!

■ No make-up!
For a natural look that'll still look good at school, go for a tint & shine lipbalm. It'll give a hint of colour and moisturise your lips at the same time.

■ Sweet Treats!
Flavoured lipglosses are double the fun — they taste as good as they look. Try fruity flavours for an instant pick-me-up!

■ Nude Is Good!
Nude shades of gloss look best with dramatic eyes. Team smoky shades with natural glossy lips for maximum impact!

Lipgloss is an obvious quick fix but for a plump pout when time is short, add extra shine to the middle of your bottom lip and opt for pink — it's a quick-fix teeth-whitener.

168

Smoky Eyes...

in 5 simple steps!

How to get your eyes glammed up with minimum effort!

Step 1:
Shadow Style

Apply dark shadow with a sponge applicator,
focusing the colour on the outer edges of your lids.
Build up the colour with a couple of applications,
winging the shade out towards the end of
your brows.

Step 2: *Blend It*

Choose a second, lighter shade of shadow and,
using your fingertips, blend the colour from the
inner corner of your eyes over the lid into the
darker shade. Apply little by little so there are no
obvious lines between your chosen colours.

Step 3: *Eyeliner*

Smoky eyes are nothing without liner! Choose a black or dark grey (if you're a first-timer!) pencil and warm it on the back of your hand so it's softer and easier to apply. Carefully line under your lower lashes and on the inner rim, and if you're feeling daring, sweep it out for cool, catty eyes!

Step 4: *Smudging*

Smudging your liner gives it that rock 'n' roll edge and it's what the smoky look's all about! Use your fingers to dab gently at the liner until it's not such a harsh line and is more an outline of your eye.

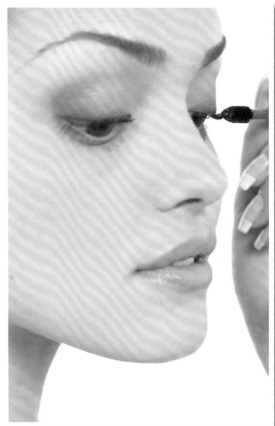

Step 5: *Mascara*

Finally, you can count on mascara to really add some glamour to your smoke-star look! Apply a coat, allow it to dry slightly then, for even more lash power, add some more! WOW!

The *Kit*...

- ■ Smoky shades of eyeshadows
- ■ Black mascara
- ■ Black or dark grey eyeliner

Wear it *with*...

- ■ Nude lips
- ■ Bronzed cheeks
- ■ Neat brows
- ■ Black or red nail polish

All products available at time of press.

173

how to...
look like
A Drama Queen!

Find out
the hot style
for you! ------------------>

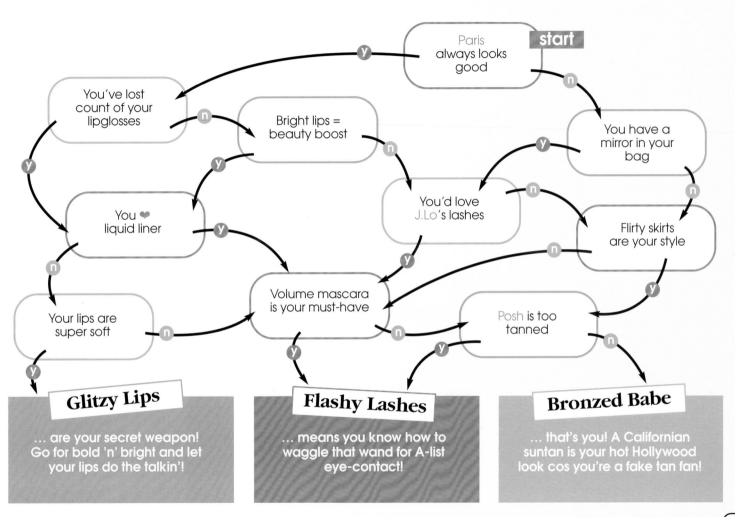

start

Paris always looks good

y → You've lost count of your lipglosses

n → You have a mirror in your bag

You've lost count of your lipglosses
- **n** → Bright lips = beauty boost
- **y** → You ❤ liquid liner

You ❤ liquid liner
- **y** → Volume mascara is your must-have
- **n** → Your lips are super soft

Bright lips = beauty boost
- **y** → You ❤ liquid liner
- **n** → You'd love J.Lo's lashes

You'd love J.Lo's lashes
- **n** → Flirty skirts are your style
- **y** → Volume mascara is your must-have

You have a mirror in your bag
- **y** → You'd love J.Lo's lashes
- **n** → Flirty skirts are your style

Flirty skirts are your style
- **n** → Volume mascara is your must-have
- **y** → Posh is too tanned

Your lips are super soft
- **n** → Volume mascara is your must-have
- **y** → **Glitzy Lips**

Volume mascara is your must-have
- **y** → **Flashy Lashes**
- **n** → Posh is too tanned

Posh is too tanned
- **y** → **Flashy Lashes**
- **n** → **Bronzed Babe**

Glitzy Lips
... are your secret weapon! Go for bold 'n' bright and let your lips do the talkin'!

Flashy Lashes
... means you know how to waggle that wand for A-list eye-contact!

Bronzed Babe
... that's you! A Californian suntan is your hot Hollywood look cos you're a fake tan fan!

how to... **FIGHT FRIZZ!**

Get the hair you've always wanted!

176

5 Steps To Sleek Style...

1. Start in the shower... use a smoothing shampoo and conditioner and gently massage into your hair. Apply a moisturising hair mask once a week and leave it on for about ten mins in the heat of your bathroom — you'll feel the difference afterwards!

2. Apply a smoothing cream and comb it through damp hair with a wide-toothed comb, starting from the ends and working up your locks.

3. Blowdry your hair on a low heat setting so as not to frazzle it, and use a nozzle on the end to direct the air down your hair and keep your look neat and sleek.

4. Apply serum to your the lengths of your hair and use what's left on your hands to smooth down the roots — don't use too much or you'll end up lookin' greasy!

5. For curly hair during hot summer months, play it safe and leave locks naturally curly — all you need is curl-styling spray to hold... Straighten your hair and you're asking for a fuzzy mane as the temperature rises!

STYLE SNIPPET!

Heat styling can wreak havoc on hair so get down to your hairdresser for a trim at least once every eight weeks to stop split ends...

Turn over for more!

STYLE SNIPPET!

Your hair can suffer in the sun and scorching holiday temperatures can cause hair to look dry and damaged — protect your locks or hide fringe frizz by sweeping hair back under a hairband or head scarf. We love the animal print versions that have hit the high street!

From Frizzy…
… To Fabulous!
Ashley Tisdale **transforms her hair!**

STYLE SNIPPET!

Eat your way to healthy hair…

● Crank up the shine factor by filling up on carrots, apricots, honey and natural yoghurt.

● Munch on cheese, seeds and nuts, which are full of protein and must-haves for healthy hair!

FRIZZ FIGHTERS:

- Smoothing shampoo and conditioner
- Wide-tooth comb
- Straightening balm
- Shine spray
- Serum
- Hair band or elastics (if all else fails!)

All products available at time of going to press.

how to...
Eat
Spaghetti!

Got a hot date and need to impress? No problem!

Things you'll need:
- Bowl of spaghetti
- Dinner fork
- Napkins (just in case!)

step 1: Hold the fork in your hand and use it to scoop up a small amount of spaghetti strands then raise it above your plate.

step 2: Make sure the spaghetti strands are completely separated from the remaining pasta on your plate.

step 3: Point the prongs of your fork towards a section of the plate that is free of pasta then quickly place the points of the fork on this section of the plate.

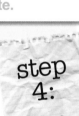

step 4: Twirl the fork to gather the spaghetti around the prongs.

step 5: With a quick scooping movement gather up the roll of pasta on your fork and place in your mouth.

Stain-free spaghetti sorted!

how... organised are you?

Clear away some mess, grab a seat and find out!

start

You always forget birthdays — y / n

Your bedroom is tidy — y / n

You've been called a dreamer — y / n

You hit the snooze button at least twice — y / n

You've gone two days without changing your underwear — y / n

You just can't decide which lad you fancy — y / n

You always keep up with the latest trends — y / n

Your homework is always done on time — y / n

You sometimes stay out too long — y / n

You know what you're wearing tomorrow — y / n

Miss Chaos!

We're surprised you managed to find your copy of *Shout 101 Things* in amongst all your dirty clothes! You're fed up of being nagged over poor timekeeping, untidiness and forgetfulness, so take control. Set time aside each day for a quick tidy up and buy a diary to jot down important events!

Miss Tidy!

OK, so you're a fairly tidy person but when it comes to timekeeping, you're often fashionably late! Why not move the time on your watch forward five minutes and then you'll always be on time! As for boys, you're still looking, but that's fine — you don't need to settle down just yet!

Miss Organised!

You're super-organised and know what you want and when you want it! You keep up-to-date with all the latest trends and have everything stored away exactly how you like it. However, doing something spontaneous can be fun — and you're allowed to make a mess now and again!

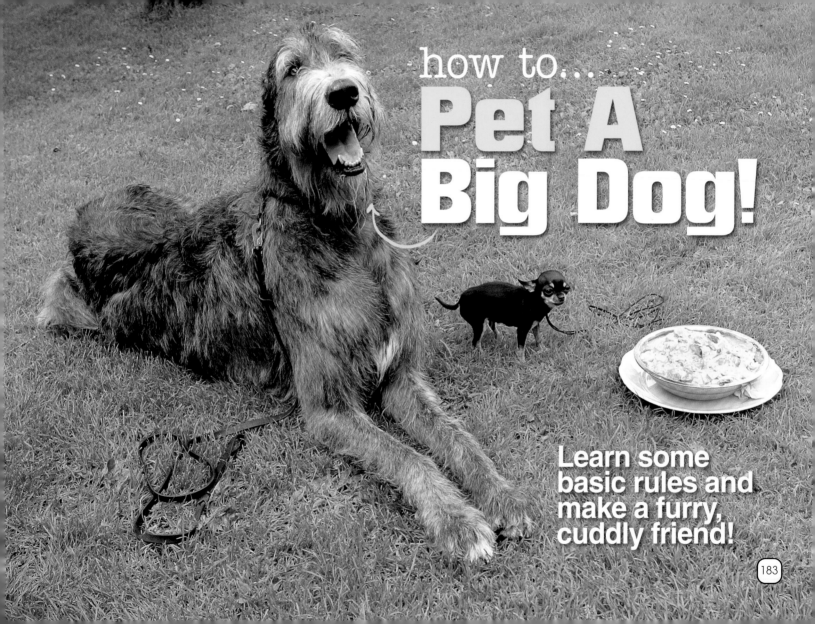

how to...
Pet A Big Dog!

Learn some basic rules and make a furry, cuddly friend!

Safety First!
- Always ask permission from the dog's owner before approaching or petting the dog.
- **Pat dogs on their chests not on the top of their heads.**
- Wait for a dog to sniff your hand before you pat or stoke it.
- **Don't act excited or noisy around dogs.**

On Their Patch!
If you're entering a dog's territory such as its home or garden…

- Rattle the gate or call out the dog's name, if you know it, or say 'good dog' in a friendly, confident voice.
- **If the dog is sleeping, try to waken it gently from a distance by calling to it.**
- Try not to move directly towards the dog — move around instead.
- **Stay well clear of a chained-up or leashed dog, as it may feel threatened.**

In the street or park
- If a dog approaches you and seems calm and friendly, let it sniff your hand.
- **If you are concerned, walk away slowly from it without making eye-contact.**
- If you have your dog with you, put it on its lead and move both of you away slowly.

FACT: This dog is called a Samoyed and is known for its huge, friendly smile!

Read The Signs!

FACT: Large dogs might look scary but breeds such as Irish Wolfhounds and St. Bernards really are just gentle giants!

An Aggressive Dog:

- Makes itself bigger by raising its hackles (the hair along its back and neck) and standing on the tips of its paws
- Lifts its lips and shows its teeth
- Barks, growls or snarls
- Has its tail raised
- Stares directly at what it's threatening

To Calm The Situation:

- Avoid eye contact
- Stand still, look down and keep your arms by your sides
- Slowly start moving away without turning your back to the dog, instead keeping side on to it

A Frightened Dog:

- Makes itself smaller by crouching or lying down
- Lays its ears flat
- Curls its tail between its legs

A Playful Dog:

- Might bark but doesn't snarl or growl
- Comes towards you then moves away from you, often kneeling down then moving back up. This is called the 'play bow' and means he's inviting you to play with him!
- Looks at you then looks away

185

how to...
handle
high
heels!

No matter how high, you can face your fear!

DO practise in your heels! Walk around your house and outside too. Practice really does make perfect! Just **DON'T** work on your walk the same day as you're wearing your heels or you'll have seriously tired tootsies!

DON'T leave the house without your plasters! Especially with new shoes, it can be difficult to judge if they'll rub and cause discomfort later on. Going prepared just means you can party longer!

DO pamper your tootsies before the big night. Paint your nails, smooth your skin and even try out a little fake tan — whatever it takes to make your feet look as fabulous as the shoes you'll be wearing!

DON'T buy shoes that are badly fitting — too big and you'll walk out of them (cringe!) but too small and you'll crush your toes — that's just asking for blisters! And no, it doesn't matter how gorgeous those stilettos are!

DO step out in heels with an ankle strap or slingback first as these will help you feel more secure in the shoe. Slip-on styles are often a bit of a challenge to walk in!

● Tennis ace Maria Sharapova is normally at home in a comfy pair of trainers but glams it up in trendy block heels

187

● **Hilary** and **Hayley Duff** make an entrance in their super-sophisticated skyscrapers

DO wear chunky heels to start off with! Skinny stiletto heels are much more difficult to walk in as you'll have less balance so try wedges or thicker heels first.

DON'T wear heels to inappropriate events... avoid tripping on cinema stairs in the dark by opting for flats but **DO** dress up with heels for parties and posh dos!

DO strike a pose! Push your hips forward, shoulders back and pull your tum in... Posture in heels is everything. You'll look elegant and instantly appear more confident — result!!

DON'T wear heels if you can't walk in them. Look at how you strut in a full length mirror and if it looks clumsy, give 'em a miss and go for flats or smaller heels until you've practised to perfection!

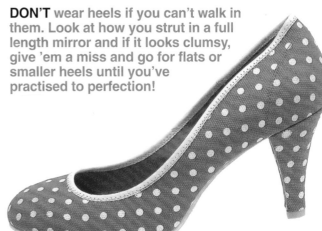

● *Iron Man star Gwyneth Paltrow* made headlines with her high heels…

All products available at time of press.

Feet Treats

1. Plasters, gel pads and anything to ease rubbing shoes

2. Cooling, soothing foot balm or moisturiser for softer soles

3. Foot wipes (or baby wipes) for instantly fresh tootsies

4. Exfoliating scrub to make dry heels a thing of the past